The EXECUTIVE

Marriage Solution

Transforming Boardroom Success into Bedroom Bliss

DR. LISA M. WEBB, MBA, MPH

*What one does is what counts. Not what
one had the intention of doing.*

—Pablo Picasso

CONTENTS

PART **1** **THE JOURNEY**

LOOKING BACK AND MOVING FORWARD

PREFACE

If you have picked up this book with the hope of finding a "quick fix" for your marriage or family relationships, then this is *not* the book for you.

Similarly, this book is not for you if you believe others are responsible for your feelings of detachment.

That said, if you want to change your circumstances at home and continue to be successful in other areas of your life, this book may be helpful — but only if you are willing to take a hard look at yourself, your behaviors, and how you are personally contributing to the challenges you face. If you are willing to take that hard look, then by all means, read this book.

Over the last few years I've worked with clients who have contemplated divorce, but turned things around instead. Throughout my twenty-five years' experience working with couples and families, I have noticed a few factors — some simple and some more complex — that promote success both in marriage and in your career. It is indeed possible to achieve balance and see all areas of your life thrive.

Again, this is not an easy proposition: it takes time and effort, as well as commitment, to succeed simultaneously in the home and at the office. On more than one occasion, I have worked with successful executives, both male and female, who found mergers and acquisitions more desirable than their investments in the health of their marriage.

The truth is that cultivating a strong family environment is hard work.

And yet, some couples tell me they believe marriage should be "easy" if the spouses are really "compatible," or if they are "soul mates." They believe that love, sex, children, or some combination thereof will be enough to sustain their relationship.

But research suggests that only 10 percent of couples maintain that intense "puppy love" years into their partnership. The reality is that for most couples, mutual effort is required to fuel the marriage. And if you refuse to buy into the idea that marriage is work, then you will be sorely disappointed.

The bottom line: if you don't act differently to improve your marriage, then nothing will be different. And that's what this book is here to do — to teach you how to do things differently. In *The Executive Marriage Solution*, I provide the tools you can use to apply the strategies that you use in business to your marriage. All that is needed in return is your commitment.

REAL-LIFE PARTNERSHIPS

An intense partnership requires nurturing and dedication. It's not unlike your physical body: without a decent diet, regular exercise, and healthy lifestyle choices, you will decay at a much faster rate.

Your marriage requires maintenance and effort. However, I've had couples say to me, "That's so unromantic. It shouldn't be work; we should be able to do this naturally if we truly love each other." What these couples do not realize is that this perspective is unsustainable. Not only that, but it is the precipitator for countless marital problems.

"Couples therapy" has a horrible track record because couples usually wait far too long to seek help. In many cases, they only make an appointment *after* their arguments have gotten out of hand and threats of divorce have either been eluded to or mentioned outright. This brings me to the goal of this book, which is not to detail the percentage of consultations that result in success — on the contrary, I want to emphasize that many spouses believe a couples approach through EMS consultation and advisement was the greatest decision they ever made.

This book is about taking a fresh look at what might need to be done to strengthen your marriage. The sooner you begin the process, the better. As my personal experience has shown, couples who do not wait until their situation becomes dire to seek help enjoy better outcomes. Rarely does seeking consultation prove fruitless, even if the spouses can only say, "This helped me realize that it wasn't going to work out between us."

TARGETS AND GOALS

Nothing is more exciting than launching an important initiative. Most executives live to check things off their lists, delegate, and make progress on new projects or product launches. At the end of the process, they experience a powerful sense of accomplishment.

But what about the time between the project execution and completion? That is the grand middle — the minutiae of the day-to-day. It's not sexy, but it is crucial to our success.

This is true of projects. And the same applies to marriage, family relationships, and life in general. The middle part is the hard part. Jeff Goins, author of *The In-Between*, reminds us that the middle is where the "important stuff" happens. Most executives I work with live in a world where they are accustomed to "getting things done," and many of these individuals have grown accustomed to seemingly instant gratification. They often "want what they want when they want it," which most often is *now*, with little tolerance for anything that is not in their power to change.

But this is not how life works. Much of life is spent waiting — waiting to get on a plane, or waiting to leave for the next important business development event. Executives spend their time waiting to get on the next conference call with shareholders, and waiting to hear if they made the quarterly projections.

It is the "middle part" that happens when you aren't waiting, but working through the projects, relationships, and events that make up 90 percent of your daily life.

Goins indicates that the "good stuff" in life is rarely behind or ahead of us, but somewhere in between. He argues that the abundant life and successful marriage you've been seeking have little to do with big events, for they tend to take shape gradually over the course of a lifetime. Indeed, to have a successful marriage, you must embrace what is called the "long game" of your relationship. You must be patient and proactive to experience the love, joy, and peace you and your spouse seek.

The tools in this book are only as effective as their implementation. Without actually following through, it is likely that very little will change in your marriage. At that point in the decision tree, you can say, "That book didn't apply to us or our family" — or you can be more truthful and say, "We were not ready to do what was needed to make positive changes."

Again, it is a bit like embarking on a new weight-loss plan. You can choose to make and sustain the changes needed to lose weight, or you can externalize your inaction by claiming, "The plan was not right for me."

There is no such thing as a quick or easy proposition. Rather, you and your spouse must make incremental changes that yield long-term dividends. This is what EMS is all about.

PLEAS FROM EXECUTIVE CLIENTS

Divorce is just as hard as — or even harder than — reconciliation. If couples can work to rebuild their marriages, only good things can come of it. My wife of thirty-five years had an affair and lived with the man, two thousand miles away, for nine months. She cited that I had "been absent for so long she wondered if I would even notice."

Yes, I noticed. And so did the other partners at my law firm. I thought I was immune to this sort of thing — I work with executives who have affairs, who are "into their careers" at the expense of their families, who come to me to "protect them and their assets" in their divorce cases. True enough, I had been gone for long hours year after year, building a very successful law firm. I thought the financial security would be enough. Clearly I missed the mark. While I was focused, motivating, articulate, and decisive at work, I was inconsiderate, preoccupied, self-centered, and lazy at home.

Rather than divorce, I forgave her when she returned. I do realize that would be hard for most to do; after all, who would want their wife back after she had physically and mentally left for almost a year? I had to get real with myself, my priorities, my values, and clue in to what mattered.

Dr. Webb's EMS was a critical part of our road to reconciliation. Due to my success with her strategies, I encourage everyone to consider reconciliation. It has worked for me and my wife. Emotions, when raw, prompt us to make unwise choices, affecting our children and ourselves. Much pain can be avoided by allowing time to reflect on life and the future. Now, having worked through that time with my family, I'm in a much better place to reflect on what happened and how I could have handled things differently. The shortest mistakes are most often the best kind — we must never allow our mistakes to evolve into bitterness or a pattern of destruction.

I have been married to my wife for over forty years now; I am sixty-eight, she sixty-three. We are living the dream, and it's because of forgiveness and reconciliation — EMS works, but only if you are willing to work as hard on it as you do on your career and other pursuits of professional success.

—JM

As my biotech company grew, I was constantly on the road with customers, press, analysts, and recruiting and energizing employees. Ultimately, over 60 percent of our revenue came from outside the U.S., and I felt it was very important to support our disparate offices that were spread across the globe. There were occasions in a given month when I was gone 50 to 75 percent of the time. Even when I was home, I was usually in a critical state of sleep deprivation and jetlag.

When I was gone, 100 percent of the daily burden fell on my spouse, usually resulting in a solid week of arguments upon my return. Then I would leave again and the cycle would continue.

After years of working full-time following the birth of our first child, and part-time after our second, my Wharton MBA wife, who had an amazing career in her own right, "decided" to become a full-time mom and take care of our children. She made this decision shortly after our third child was born — and I use the word "decided" because at the time, it was clear to both of us that I wasn't willing to be a 50/50 partner at home. My wife endured the rocky years while I established the business, but we both knew we had to reevaluate and recalibrate when we sold out to a pharmaceutical company.

The sale afforded enough profit that I could stay home for twelve to eighteen months. I had grown tired of my wife's complaints that she felt like the "lone ranger." Frankly, I was a self-serving asshole who thought I could come home and run things better than my wife ever could — after all, she had just been a stay-at-home mom, so how hard could it be?

After two months of packing lunches, driving carpools, and making dinners, it had also become glaringly obvious that our marriage was strained and we did not feel connected anymore. I learned about Dr.

Webb and EMS from a physician colleague who had confided he was having some of the same issues when he finally finished his MD/PhD residency.

Over the next six months, I worked with Dr. Webb, checked my ego, and realized that I did not have all the answers. It was then that I began doing real work in the family. My wife and I mapped the plan for our future through EMS. Although we always made an effort to be real with each other, I can say we probably would have landed in mediation or divorce without EMS. And now that my startup has become successful, and I am working toward success at home, I genuinely believe I could have coached my former CEO self to succeed in both places if only I knew what I do now. This work is hardly easy. And yet, if you are both willing to change your marriage, EMS can be a powerful approach.

—BB

I am a CTO of a major health services corporation. As a female executive, I am always "in charge" and feel like I have to prove my worth, as I am the only woman in company leadership. We came to Dr. Webb on the verge of divorce after I had an emotional affair with a colleague I traveled with often. My husband and I had been working with a relationship coach for four months, and we fought after every session. I was at the end of my rope because of all the stress and anger I felt. This was what led to my emotional affair in the first place.

We were unable to communicate in a way that made me feel like my husband really understood my concerns and pain. I couldn't trust him to be a committed and invested partner in our marriage — in fact, I did not feel like we were even in the same marriage.

Dr. Webb's style, technique, and experience with other executives helped to put us both at ease. Her blunt and matter-of-fact approach allowed us to feel hopeful while addressing the facts and situations that needed to change. In no way did she take sides, give the answers, or tell us what to do. Instead, she gave us the education we needed to understand the key differences in our personalities and what we were doing to escalate the conflict between us. The fighting ultimately stopped, and my husband and I began to talk to each other in new ways. We both felt heard.

In four weeks, I began to experience feelings of love for my husband again. We worked with Dr. Webb for six months and not only felt the renewal of love, but my husband and I also began to really understand each other in ways we had not known before. EMS enabled me to see how I was escalating our conflicts and pushing my husband away. We literally went from divorce court to having another baby and reviving our love and marriage.

EMS is not for the faint of heart, but your relationship will change for the better. Give this approach a try and you will not be disappointed.

—ST

I hope you take my clients' words to heart, and keep them in mind while you read this book. The hard work it takes to sustain a marriage is an investment, but in many cases, the returns are astounding.

INTRODUCTION

Contrary to what you may think, the Executive Marriage Solution is not a quick fix. It is not another way to say "therapy" or "relationship coaching." Rather, it is a system designed to give couples the tools they need to address the problems in their marriage, and strengthen the bond between them. These tools are presented to each couple by a trusted relationship advisor — but we'll get to that.

EMS applies proven business strategies in the context of a relationship. Far too many executives burn out at home, often because they devote so much time to their work. Their spouses say they are fed up, but the executives don't know what to do. They already feel trapped by the pressure of their work, and feel they don't have the energy to be an attentive partner.

A HYBRID APPROACH

If both parties agree to put in the time and effort needed to repair their marriage, then the couple can salvage their relationship. However, therapy is not necessarily the answer. While some aspects of therapy could be of benefit, marriage counseling if often a last-ditch effort in response to an ultimatum of sorts — a threat that "something has to change."

Similarly, relationship coaching can be worthwhile for certain marital and relationship issues. Relationship coaching, however, is often viewed as an early intervention. It can present a number of effective listening and communication strategies, but the spouses won't necessarily implement them. You see, most couples are not particularly self-aware early in their relationship; some believe most of their issues are transient, and can be resolved without truly addressing them.

EMS is a hybrid approach, and combines the benefits of relationship strategy, change management, and organizational development. During the EMS journey, I serve as the couple's trusted relationship advisor, not unlike a business advisor.

THE IMPORTANCE OF TRUST

Merriam-Webster defines trust as "assured reliance on the character, ability, strength, or truth of someone or something." But the term *trusted advisor* has a relatively loose definition in the business world.

Just as many professionals boast that they are trusted advisors to their clients, a ***trusted relationship advisor*** is impartial to the "politics" of your marriage and family. Your trusted relationship advisor is an unbiased expert in strengthening relationships.

One author has detailed the attributes of a "trusted advisor."[1] Research shows that the more we trust an individual, the more they can help us improve our lives.[2] The stronger the relationship, the more likely a client is to heed the advisor's advice. I have applied the traits of a trusted advisor to the context of a relationship:

1. THE TRUSTED RELATIONSHIP ADVISOR UNDERSTANDS THAT THIS IS ABOUT YOU.

A trusted relationship advisor is a genuine, real person. Transparency is critical to strengthening your relationship. Rather than paying a relationship advisor to make you feel good, you are paying for guidance in order to improve your marriage.

2. THE TRUSTED RELATIONSHIP ADVISOR IS CREDIBLE.

Professionally, I have worked with hundreds of executive couples and families over more than twenty years. This experience has afforded my practice a decent-sized cross-section from which to generalize, allowing us to implement proven strategies rooted in real client cases.

---

1   Green, C. H., Galford, R. M., & Maister, D. H. (2001). *The Trusted Advisor*. Simon and Schuster.

2   Johnson, D., & Grayson, K. (2005). Cognitive and affective trust in service relationships. *Journal of Business research, 58(4),* 500-507.

3. THE TRUSTED RELATIONSHIP ADVISOR CONNECTS ON AN EMOTIONAL LEVEL.

Couples may decide to work on their marriage, but doing so won't necessarily drive them to take action. Building an emotional connection with clients promotes an understanding of each other's values, and presents deep insights into what drives behaviors and patterns in the relationship.

4. THE TRUSTED RELATIONSHIP ADVISOR BELIEVES IN LONG-TERM IMPROVEMENTS.

Are your strongest relationships the ones you have had the longest? Feedback from clients I have worked with indicates that their main priority is to feel understood and valued. I am pleased to say that over 50 percent of our clientele has come from word-of-mouth recommendations. This reinforces our focus on building long-term relationships over making short-term gains.

Now that we have gone over the concept of a trusted relationship advisor, we can delve completely into the text. I genuinely hope the Executive Marriage Solution — the concept detailed in the book — will give you the impetus to take action, come up with a plan, and ultimately strengthen your marriage with a trusted relationship advisor by your side.

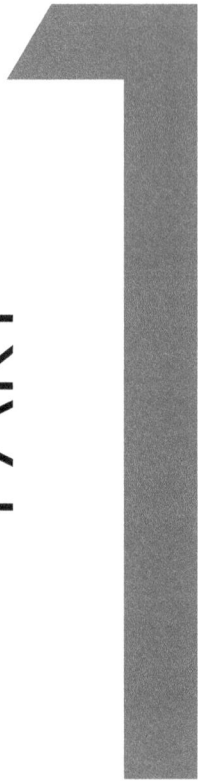

PART 1

THE JOURNEY
LOOKING BACK AND MOVING FORWARD

1 HOW DID YOU GET HERE?

*There are no accidents
... There is only some
purpose that we haven't
yet understood.*

—Deepak Chopra

Spouses in executive marriages tell me there is something unique about their bond. One executive recounts:

I am a serial entrepreneur and have been the CEO of several successful startups in the health technology arena. It has become more apparent that many of my struggles

9

as a CEO are surprisingly common. One observation that stands out — probably because it is rarely discussed — is how many founder/CEOs have relationship struggles with their significant others and families. My brightest years at the startup were my darkest years at home.

We all lead busy lives. So busy, in fact, that most of us find ourselves hurrying about, snatching the rare moment with our spouse and family. We might long for a simpler lifestyle — one where we can truly connect — and yet the executive lifestyle makes it difficult. There is a great deal of pressure, and simply not enough time in the day.

AT WHAT COST?

Research suggests that 90 percent of CEOs struggle with "work-life balance."[3] Granted, we must make sacrifices while climbing the executive ladder, but taking this too far can yield dire consequences. If you don't make time to cultivate your marriage and family connections, the foundation of these relationships may very well crumble.

In *The New Secrets of CEOs: 200 Global Chief Executives on Leading*, researchers interviewed 150 chief executives about the impact of their professional roles on their personal lives and overall health.[4] The authors found that CEOs primarily experienced emotions such as frustration, disappointment, irritation, and overwhelm outside the office.

At the root of these feelings are internal conflict and a lack of equilibrium. When a person fulfills the role of a global chief executive,

---

3   *Tappin, S., & Cave, A. (2010). The new secrets of CEOs: 200 global chief executives on leading. London: Nicholas Brealey.*
4   *Ibid.*

they must determine how to foster relationships — and in many cases, care for their family — without sacrificing their workplace responsibilities. Some executives have a difficult time achieving any semblance of work-life equilibrium, which can result in dire emotional consequences.

Sally, for instance, is a busy executive with a demanding work schedule. She and her husband Bob are struggling to navigate their own executive marriage.

CASE STUDY — SALLY AND BOB

Sally logs long hours at a financial services firm. She travels considerably for her position, which she loves. She and her husband, along with their two children, have moved six times in the last ten years for her career. It feels to Bob like their lives revolve entirely around Sally's job.

Each time Bob asks Sally for a "simpler life" or "more home stability," Sally grows impatient. Bob has told her he feels like one of her employees, not her husband, and that things need to change.

But Sally becomes angry when Bob asks for more of her time. Her excuses indicate that she is too busy, as Sally works late into the evening and on weekends. She resents her husband's nagging over her jam-packed schedule.

Meanwhile, Bob believes that Sally thinks a little bit of time here and there is enough to sustain their marriage — no matter that he has begun to feel unimportant, cast aside, and abandoned. He expresses that his love for his wife is slowly dying.

What This Means

A great deal of research has been conducted on couples like Sally and Bob. Scientific literature is fraught with studies that detail the health ramifications of living in a state of such conflict. If you experience feelings such as frustration or overwhelm for more than 80 percent of the day, you risk experiencing an increase in stress and cortisol in your body, which can lead to accelerated aging, heart attacks, and even cancer.[5] Accordingly, while you are in an executive role, you must accept the limitations in your life outside work. These limitations include the potential strain on your health, happiness, family, and relationships.

Consider the following. Most of my executive clients are a bit older when they marry, but the odds are often stacked against their marriages succeeding. In fact, the National Center for Health Statistics revealed that 50 percent of all marriages involving brides aged 25 and older ultimately fail.[6][7] This poses a major risk not only for couples, but also for families with one or both parents working in an executive role.

In business, a failure rate of 50 percent would raise some serious concerns. But for millions of married couples, divorce has become a routine way out of a difficult situation. Oftentimes, a default ap-

---

5   *McCraty, R., Barrios-Choplin, B., Rozman, D., Atkinson, M., & Watkins, A. D. (1998). The impact of a new emotional self-management program on stress, emotions, heart rate variability, DHEA and cortisol. Integrative Physiological and Behavioral Science, 33(2), 151–170.*

6   *Centers for Disease Control and Prevention, National Center for Health Statistics. (2012). First marriages in the United States: Data from the 2006–2010 National Survey of Family Growth. US Department of Health and Human Services.*

7   *Martin, T. C., & Bumpass, L. L. (1989). Recent trends in marital disruption. Demography, 26(1), 37–51.*

proach is to throw around the idea of divorcing as a "cry for help." This effort is most often intended to draw the spouse's attention to the fact that something is wrong, or not working in the relationship. Divorce, however, should not be brought up casually if you are hoping to repair your marriage.

This is because with divorce at the back of your mind, you risk feeling conflicted while trying to work through your differences.[8] You may wonder whether your relationship is even worth repairing, which is not a productive outlook if you hope to create positive change.

The same thing applies to couples with children. These individuals must consider how the tension in their lives affects their family environment.[9] Children pick up on their parents' stress, so it's important to be open and communicative with your loved ones. Focus not only on the problem, but also on what you hope to solve in your relationships outside the office.

MOST PROBLEMS ARE SOLVABLE

Many couples consider an intervention a "success" if it helps them salvage their marriage. When most couples arrive for help, they believe that meeting with a third-party is a last-ditch effort to repair their bond. Others want an outside source — the coach, psychologist, or doctor — to *tell* them whether to dissolve their relationship. Perhaps there are feelings of guilt about "doing what's right for the children," and the couple wants an unbiased professional

---

8   Fein, E., & Schneider, S. (2007). *The Rules (TM) for marriage: Time-tested secrets for making your marriage work.* New York, NY: Grand Central.
9   Roth, K. E., Harkins, D. A., & Eng, L. A. (2014). *Parental conflict during divorce as an indicator of adjustment and future relationships: A retrospective sibling study. Journal of Divorce & Remarriage, 55(2), 117-138.*

to confirm that divorce is the best decision they can make for their family.

Studies show the primary factors leading to divorce are poor communication, nagging, and lack of affection.[10] While some might assume that addiction and abuse are typically at play, it is often the little things that add up and eventually culminate in divorce. What this means, however, is that most unhappy marriages can improve. It reveals that they are worth changing. This is especially enlightening for couples with children, as it can help them maintain a stable family environment.

To drive positive change, the first step is to incorporate good manners into your communication. Conservatively, I would say that 80 percent of couples seeking my assistance talk over each other when they are in my office. If they clearly lack respect for each other in front of a stranger, then I have little faith that they do things differently at home.

I tend to address this problem in a number of ways. First, I set a ground rule, and state that only one person can speak at a time. Usually, one or both parties will then launch into all the grievances that led them to seek consultation. And while I may allow this to go on for a few minutes, I ultimately express that each spouse should describe what they desire for the future rather than look in the rearview mirror.

This is a central principle behind EMS — for couples to focus on what they want their relationship to look like instead of poring over the issues that brought them to my office in the first place.

---

10 Hetherington, E. M., Cox, M., & Cox, R. (1985). *Long-term effects of divorce and remarriage on the adjustment of children. Journal of the American Academy of Child Psychiatry, 24(5), 518–530.*

Look at your relationship from a business perspective. Would a company cut their entire product line if, after years of success, they experienced two quarters of negative growth? Possibly, but in most cases the corporate office would strategize opportunities to get the product back on track. This would likely involve some root cause analysis into how the current situation came to be. Maybe the change was the result of a marketing or branding decision, or even an evolving target demographic.

FOREVER CHANGED

In my opinion, marriages cannot be "saved"; rather, each couple can divorce their old marriage and begin a new one with the same partner. This is a healthy outlook, as it indicates both spouses are on the same team and working toward a common goal. And as I mentioned previously, families can take this unified approach to promote patience, empathy, and strong communication within their unit.

Cindy and Tony took this approach to start fresh, renew their bond, and ultimately strengthen their marriage.

CASE STUDY — CINDY AND TONY

Cindy and Tony had been together for fifteen years, and married for three when they came to see me. Although I had seen Cindy for executive coaching several times in the past, we had not yet addressed her relationship concerns. In fact, Tony initiated the consult, as three days before Cindy had said she was "done" with the marriage, moved out, and gotten her own apartment. Tony indicated he was clueless as to what made Cindy feel this way; he did not understand what could possibly have gone so wrong that she would walk out on their relationship.

The spouses met when Cindy was in medical school and Tony was a practicing architect at his own firm. In the beginning, they were in alignment with what they wanted in their relationship. They were both content to be home when Cindy was not at the library studying. Then their bond shifted. Tony was happy with the way things were and did not desire to grow his firm. In contrast, Cindy was appointed Chief Medical Officer at a local hospital, with growing responsibilities. She was excited about the direction her career was taking, but frustrated when she would come home from a fourteen-hour shift to find Tony on the couch.

But Tony was grappling with his own life stressors. He was despondent and depressed, having recently placed his mother in a nursing facility for Alzheimer's disease. He had also lost two major clients, both considerable sources of revenue for the firm, and had no choice but to lay off two long-term employees. Mounting debt and fear of losing his business sent him down a path of discouragement. He got shingles and began experiencing panic and anxiety to the point where he did not want to leave the house. He had taken up residence on the couch, and it was all he could do to get up and go to work.

Cindy asked Tony to go to galas and executive dinners as her plus-one, but he told her he hated "those sorts of functions." Over time, Cindy became more withdrawn from Tony. She stopped asking him to go with her to social events, and Tony grew relieved. But Cindy was always on the phone, making plans with other people, and communication between the spouses became very transactional — what to eat for dinner, when to make the monthly mortgage payment, etc. One day Cindy called from a business trip and told Tony she wasn't coming home.

Tony flew into a rage. He texted and called Cindy incessantly, accusing her of having an affair. He wanted to know "why" she'd really left.

The spouses, however, could not have a civil conversation over the phone because it would quickly escalate into an argument. The one time Cindy did come by the house when Tony was there, the exchange turned heated. Tony pinned his wife into a corner and smashed her phone to express how angry he was — at her, at their life, and at their marriage. From that point on, Cindy refused to go to the house when Tony was there.

I saw both spouses individually for some time. Cindy maintained that she "wanted space" and "was done." Tony remained genuinely confused about how their relationship had gotten to this place.

But over the next five weeks, he backed off. He stopped calling Cindy and no longer asked her when she was coming home. He began working on himself and realized how dependent he had become on his wife. In fact, Cindy had taken charge of everything in their home — she oversaw their finances, groceries, laundry, and everything else. Tony was lost when she walked out. I encouraged him to figure out whether their marriage was really healthy. Over time, Tony discovered that he didn't miss Cindy — he missed having her at home, and yearned for the relationship they'd had before she began her new position at the hospital.

When Cindy moved out, she too started to grieve the loss of the relationship. She came to see me for an individual consult and told me she had not yet filed for divorce. Whenever she thought about going to the attorney's office, she became immobilized. She did not know what she wanted for the future, and I gave her the analogy of her relationship dying a slow death. I told Cindy that she owed it to herself and Tony to make a decision.

"But what if I'm making the worst mistake of my life?" she asked me. "I can't decide what to do."

The evolution of a relationship, I explained, is similar to a disease that would be terminal if left untreated. The body changes while coping with a potentially fatal condition, and so it is with marriage.

Cindy could decide to let the cancer of past behaviors continue to dominate her bond with Tony. This would, in effect, sign a "do not resuscitate" order for their relationship.

Conversely, she and Tony could decide to change their marriage for the better by undergoing "treatment" — that is, EMS — without any presupposed notion that their relationship would survive.

Just like Cindy and Tony's marriage depended on a mutual decision to seek treatment, so does your relationship. You must decide whether to dissolve your marriage or attempt to resuscitate whatever might be left of it. Throughout this book, I will give you the tools to guide the course of your relationship.

KEY TAKEAWAYS

- The primary complaints leading to divorce are poor communication, lack of affection, and nagging.

- Most problems are solvable, and the decision to resuscitate your marriage is well within your power.

- But with the prospect of divorce at the back of your mind, you will likely feel conflicted while working through your differences. It is important to be objective, and focus on what you want for the future rather than what took place in the past.

NEXT UP

Couples must work together to cultivate strong relationships. Both spouses are involved in the process, and everyone should do their part to make unifying choices. The following chapter details how executives can use their business skills to break down walls and build bridges within their marriage or family unit

2 BREAK WALLS AND BUILD BRIDGES

We build too many walls and not enough bridges.

—Isaac Newton

I can say with confidence that very few couples begin their marriage with divorce in mind. Most relationships start out with both partners feeling happy and secure.

However, spouses in a successful marriage must manage their conflicting viewpoints. The way couples handle the tension between them will determine whether the relationship becomes constructive or destructive.

This is because your circumstances are a direct result of the decisions you make. Just as there is no manual on how to find stability in your life as a high-ranking executive, there is no guide on how to maintain a successful marriage. But you can make the decision to break the walls in your relationship and build bridges instead. The following case study will show you how to accomplish this.

CASE STUDY — BRIAN AND KIM

When Brian's friend offered to include him in a new business venture, Kim felt strongly that he should stay at his current job — a steady role that generated considerable income. But Brian was bored with his position as CIO of a financial services firm and wanted a new challenge. He and Kim were constantly fighting, and they both started to contemplate divorce. There was clearly a wall between them in their relationship.

Neither spouse felt "understood" or "heard" in the marriage. Brian believed Kim saw him as "just a paycheck," and that she didn't care whether he was happy. This also confused Brian, since Kim had supported him in the past.

The backstory: Brian had always been the entrepreneurial type. Over the course of his twenty-five-year marriage with Kim, he served as both a venture capitalist and CEO of a number of businesses. Brian's income fluctuated greatly, but he didn't mind borrowing money to live on when times were lean. Kim was more conservative. After working as the Executive Director of a local non-profit for many years, she was looking forward to retiring with a small pension. But while Brian and Kim had paid off their home, they didn't have much in savings.

Both spouses had valid points to support their arguments, and felt they were at an impasse. Before coming to me, Brian had threatened to "go ahead and start the new venture with or without [Kim]." This would have been destructive to their relationship, done little to build a bridge in their marriage, and instead thickened the wall between them.

For Brian and Kim to build a bridge between their perspectives, they needed to establish a couple of foundational elements:

1. They needed to commit to the relationship for anything to change. The word "divorce" is like salt causing a car to rust in the winter in that it reveals a *lack* of commitment.

Cars do not rust immediately — the process happens slowly, eroding the metal undercarriage and creeping up the body of the vehicle. Likewise, the word divorce erodes whatever is left of the relationship. It takes on a life of its own, and left untreated, it zaps all motivation for building a bridge.

2. The couple needed to recognize that they were on the "same team," and that Kim did in fact care about Brian's happiness. While she was fearful for the future, she loved and supported her husband.

Once Brian understood that Kim wanted him to be happy — that she knew he grew bored easily and had a knack for business ventures, yet she wanted to feel secure — the spouses were able to build a bridge.

The house was the most important thing to Kim. She viewed it as security and believed that as long as she had the property and her pension, everything would be okay. To insulate the house from any future business claims, Brian and Kim decided to transfer the title to Kim exclusively. By doing so, they tore down the wall between them and built a bridge, which made the spouses feel more comfortable going forward with their marriage.

CONSIDER WHAT YOU WANT TO BUILD

The strongest, most longstanding relationships have one thing in common: a willingness to share and acknowledge different viewpoints in a respectful environment. Serene settings like a weekend getaway or a couples retreat can foster healthier communication. Since stress can cloud our thoughts, many couples like to invest in a change of scenery to begin working on their marriage.

One opportunity to engage in this relationship investment is through an EMS individualized weekend 1:1 overhaul, or in a group relationship consultation in which three couples collaborate and work through their relationship issues with an experienced facilitator. It is in situations like these that you and your mate can take action, implement the EMS framework in a practical environment, and improve your marriage.

Couples can improve their interpersonal skills and make the decision to turn their differences into opportunities — or they can harbor resentment and build a sprawling, insurmountable wall. The issue here is that if the wall becomes too tall, the spouses will grow even further apart, and eventually one or both partners will no longer *want* to overcome the challenges in their relationship.

To that end, research reveals it is not uncommon for couples to spend years building walls instead of bridges. This is why couples married ten or more years have experienced the most significant spike in the divorce rate.[11] Moreover, it is not uncommon for couples twenty-five or thirty years into their marriages to get divorced.[12]

Any number of things can influence the deterioration of a relationship. One researcher described four negative patterns that predict divorce and other relationship destroyers: blame, defensiveness, contempt, and stonewalling.[13] These behaviors exist not only in marriage, but in every relationship. And when they become the norm rather than an occasional negative interaction, these patterns can make relationships toxic.

---

11   *Centers for Disease Control and Prevention, National Center for Health Statistics. (2012). First marriages in the United States: Data from the 2006–2010 National Survey of Family Growth. US Department of Health and Human Services.*

12   *Cherlin, A. (2009). Marriage, divorce, remarriage. Cambridge, MA: Harvard University Press.*

13   *Gottman, J. M. (2014). What predicts divorce?: The relationship between marital processes and marital outcomes. Hove, UK: Psychology Press.*

But these patterns don't have to be the norm. The following communication tips promote positive interactions:

- Instead of blaming your spouse, consider their perspective.

- Instead of feeling defensive, open yourself up to new information without jumping to conclusions.

- Instead of feeling contempt, think about why you respect and appreciate your partner.

- Instead of stonewalling your spouse, embrace their vulnerability. Give them the opportunity to understand what you are thinking without casting their thoughts aside.

When people uncover the power of their actions, they can choose to change their behaviors and strengthen their marriage. One authority on divorce and domestic relations claims lack of communication is the main cause of divorce in longstanding marriages.[14] This authority further states that in many relationships, a couple's sheer inability to speak honestly with each other hinders their ability to connect. Rather than baring their souls and treating each other like best friends, some spouses focus on the superficial components of their relationship. The problem here is that they risk talking *through* each other rather than *to* each other.

And the destruction rarely ends there. In some cases, lack of communication may lead to drinking, infidelity, or even abuse.[15] For this reason, among others, healthy communication is especially important in relationships where children are involved.

---

14 Glieberman, H. A. (1981). *Why so many marriages fail. US News & World Report, 7, p. 54.*

15 *Ibid*

Do you consider this viewpoint dated? Perhaps you believe it is not a true reflection of reality. My experience indicates the contrary. I have found many relationships are so bogged down with negativity that the couple starts to believe poor communication is in fact healthy, and indicative of a solid bond.

Granted, spouses coping with marital strain know they are at an impasse. Most people are aware they are going through difficult times, even when they struggle to articulate the challenges they face. This is precisely why so many couples come to see me — they recognize they are having problems, but do not know when or how they built the wall between them.

To demolish barriers in their relationship, the couple and I work to pinpoint the lack of tolerance that is causing the spouses to drift apart. Oftentimes, they repress their feelings of discomfort, and fail to recognize that neither person is perfect. When we forget our loved ones are only human, bitterness and resentment ensue.

In every marriage — in nearly every important relationship — we do things that hurt the people we love most. This is inevitable, because no one is perfect. And in some cases, spouses repeat the same mistakes over and over again, even after they confront each other on their behavior.

SPREADING OF TOXICITY

What do a piece of moldy bread and termites have in common? In both items, the presenting problem is generally not representative of the entire issue.

Have you ever examined a piece of moldy bread? At first glance, it looks like there is only one contaminated area. Under a micro-

scope, however, you would see the long roots of the mold spreading throughout the slice. You might also look at a termite-infested home in this way — while the exterior appears to be the problem, the interior is compromised as well. The presenting issue is not representative of the whole situation.

Bitterness develops the same way. A single wave of bitterness can spread through the heart and infect your entire body. If you wait too long to address it, the negativity will manifest in your attitude, demeanor, and even your health.

What is the source of this resentment? Bitterness results from embracing feelings of hurt and refusing to forgive the person you believe to be responsible for your pain. Most of the time, bitterness is the product of relatively small-scale actions — lack of understanding, financial misuse, harsh comments — that accumulate over time. Each offense takes residence in the heart, and at some point, you can no longer cope. As such, it is when you are overwhelmed that bitterness can cause the most damage.

And if you don't tackle your resentment, the damage can be quite widespread. In addition to your marriage, bitterness can affect your children. It's contagious, not to mention capable of generating a great deal of strain in your family relationships.

It is no secret that one person's criticisms can make others more critical as well — and bitterness is no different. By working on your resentment, you can help others tackle their own negativity. Ultimately, while you may feel there is little hope for your marriage, it is never too late to focus on rebuilding your family.

LONELINESS AT THE TOP

Because of their professional success, many executives struggle to accept challenges in their relationships. Perhaps they fail to understand the reason for their appointment with me. If the executive is so successful professionally, they may wonder how their marital issues could possibly have anything to do with them?

One study revealed that executives find their positions intensely lonely, with no pool of trusted confidants to turn to during stressful times.[16] From a distance, one might think spouses and family members are the first people executives would confide in during challenging times. In my clinical experience, however, many higher-level executives consider family a stressor in itself. Some find it simpler to keep home and work completely separate, as they believe mixing the two is "one more thing to do," and they are "already exhausted."

This is a selfish approach to marital communication. People do not get married or enter a long-term relationship to be an island unto themselves. Nevertheless, many executives take this approach, often citing they prefer not to share too much with their loved ones because they "don't want them to worry." The internalization of work stress damages the couple's intimacy, often resulting in anger and instability.

Since irritable people tend to blow minor grievances out of proportion, they may have a tendency to end relationships rather than put

---

16 Tappin, S., & Cave, A. (2010). *The new secrets of CEOs: 200 global chief Executives on leading.* London: Nicholas Brealey.

in the work needed to resolve their problems. Consequently, they often alienate themselves from others — even their own families — because they do not hold themselves accountable for the issues they are facing.[17]

In many cases, these individuals decide the solution to their problems lies outside their marriage. Some seek out an extramarital affair instead of working to resolve their communication issues.

Of course, affairs do not simply happen. They are the product of our decision-making, and occur in phases over time.

PHASES OF AN AFFAIR

Consider the executive who doesn't want to "worry" their spouse, and therefore refuses to confide in them. This can cause emotional distance in the relationship and ultimately lead to an affair.

PHASE 1: EMOTIONAL READINESS AND VULNERABILITY

One spouse is open to subtle temptations, which basically opens the door for another person to enter the marriage. This stage is best addressed by recognizing the problem, and by having both spouses reinvest their energy back into the relationship.

PHASE 2: AWARENESS AND RENDEZVOUS

If the spouses do not escape the first phase, they risk proceeding to the second phase of the affair process. Perhaps one spouse occasionally thinks about someone else, and innocent thoughts turn

---

17   Carter, L., & Minirth, F. (2004). *The Anger Trap: Free yourself from the frustrations that sabotage your life. Jossey-Bass.*

into fantasy. This may lead to dreaming about the other person or masturbating while fantasizing about them.

This fantasy crosses into reality when the disloyal spouse schedules a rendezvous with the individual — often under the guise of cultivating a friendship. This is why the disloyal partner often justifies the bond to their spouse by saying, "You're crazy! So-and-so and I are just friends."

The other person then begins to meet the disloyal spouse's basic human needs — needs they haven't let their husband or wife meet in quite some time. Perhaps they start an affair with someone who seems to understand their work in a way they feel their spouse never could.

Around the other person, the disloyal spouse enjoys a serotonin pleasure rush akin to being high on drugs. The adrenaline of the forbidden encounters and secret cell phone is intoxicating, and so the affair begins.

PHASE 3: DISCOVERY

At this stage, the loyal spouse becomes aware of the affair. They are devastated, and then start doing things that would under normal circumstances go against their character. A warm, empathetic wife might slap her husband; the spouse who prefers to avoid confrontation might appear at his partner's house for a fight. During this time, the disloyal spouse is usually defensive, elusive, and upset.

PHASE 4: STAY OR GO

In the final phase of an affair, the married couple must decide whether they want to stay together.

Most affairs end in about two years. Some culminate in a nasty divorce with a great deal of animosity, but not without regret. According to one researcher, 80 percent of those who divorce during an affair regret their decision.[18] If the disloyal spouse chooses to leave the marriage, the affair usually ends as well, as most fantasies crumble beneath the weight of "real life."

Others attempt to marry their partner in the affair, but this is an anomaly. Statistics suggest that less than 10 percent of unfaithful spouses wed the person with whom they had an affair, and that over 75 percent of these unions end in divorce.

A number of affairs end when the loyal spouse encourages the disloyal spouse to cease all contact with the other person. During this time, the disloyal spouse may experience withdrawal-like symptoms where the pleasure of the affair is absent. It is during this time that the disloyal spouse must realize the affair was a fantasy reaction to boredom or stress, and focus on rebuilding their marriage.

What would that look like? Read Joyce and Fred's case study to find out.

CASE STUDY — JOYCE AND FRED

Joyce and Fred made an appointment for a consultation after Joyce uncovered her husband's affair. She was devastated about the betrayal, as she and Fred had been married for twenty years. Fred worked as Vice President of Operations at a large multinational company, and traveled several times a year to oversee the regional plants.

---

18 *Hawkins, A. J., & Fackrell, T. A. (2011). Should I Keep Trying To Work It Out? Sacred and Secular Perspectives on the Crossroads of Divorce. Brigham Young University Studies, 50(2), 143-157.*

Everything seemed fine during my initial evaluation of the couple. Joyce and Fred did not argue incessantly. They had a robust intimate life. Their three children were teenagers, and did not impose unnecessary strife on the family. The couple had a number of mutual friends; they were also active in their church and considered a model couple by many in their parish.

A former healthcare practitioner, Joyce no longer worked outside the home. She and Fred were financially stable and did not appear to have any glaring marital issues. Consequently, she was shocked to find that things were not as they had seemed.

During our consultation, Fred maintained that the affair "just happened" — that it was "just sex" and certainly "not planned." Three conjoint sessions led to a circuitous lack of progress. The couple struggled to communicate. Joyce believed that since the affair happened once, it would happen again. Fred firmly disagreed.

But the affair itself should not have been their point of focus. Rather, Fred and Joyce needed to get to the root of the issue.

You see, the "why" is a critical aspect of an affair. Affairs do not "just happen," and they do not occur in a vacuum with only one spouse responsible. The choices we make, and the consequences of these choices, are what determine whether we build a bridge or a wall in our relationships. The fourth session, Fred came to the appointment by himself. Joyce had a prior commitment, so I focused on Fred specifically during our time together. We discussed his executive position, the stressors he experienced as a result of his job, his confidants at work, and other career-related details.

Fred admitted that he felt Joyce did not understand him. Over the years, he had internalized his stress because he felt it was "too much to explain" to Joyce. He feared his wife would not understand the context of his work life, and admitted to yearning for a relationship where he would not have to "explain every detail" of the crises he managed, the cultural differences he had to navigate across continents, and other aspects of the business that were commonplace to him and his associates.

His colleagues "got it" in a way that Joyce did not, Fred explained. Then he confided that one of his work associates was the woman with whom he'd had the affair.

I asked Fred, "How can Joyce possibly 'get it' if you don't take the time to let her into your world?"

He admitted, "Letting her in was another exhaustion . . . another thing to do." He felt it was easier to bring in the paycheck and avoid talking about his stress. Joyce would not worry if he "seemed okay," which Fred thought would help improve their home life.

Fred claimed that the relationship with the paramour was "easy" and that he did not "[have] to explain everything" because she simply "got it." Over time he and his associate had "become close," and eventually they consummated their relationship. He claimed the act took place on a business trip, after drinking too much at the end of a long workday.

One part of our session stood out to me. Fred was fixated on the fact that the physical affair had only happened once. "Why couldn't Joyce move beyond it?" he wondered.

I explained that since Fred had discussed intimate matters with the other woman, Joyce felt left out — no matter that his conversations with the other woman revolved around work. In Joyce's eyes,

Fred was fostering a stronger bond with his associate than the bond he had with his own wife. And although he had only slept with the other woman once, he had been intimate with her in his mind on many occasions. He had even thought of her while having sex with Joyce.

And yet, he maintained that he "only had actual sex with her once."

I asked Fred if Joyce knew about his emotional connection with the other woman. He said he didn't find it "relevant," but I countered that Joyce would find it very relevant. In actuality, discussing the emotions behind the affair would help Fred and Joyce sift through the challenges in their marriage.

The following week, we decided that Fred would discuss his emotional connection with the other woman. It was important, I believed, for him to speak honestly with his wife and determine whether Joyce felt the sexual exploit was of more consequence than his longer-term emotional affair.

So Fred explained that he had known the other woman for four years, and that he often discussed business with her instead of "bringing it home." He admitted that he loved Joyce "very much," but that "it was hard to explain everything about work" to her.

Once again, Joyce was devastated. She had a difficult time processing the fact that this woman had actually been a fixture in her marriage for four years, even though she and Fred had only consummated their relationship once.

- Clearly, Fred and Joyce made a series of choices over the course of their relationship that culminated in the extramarital affair. Fred made the choice not to divulge his work life to Joyce because he "didn't want to make her upset."

- Fred made the choice not to explain the details of his work because he found it "exhausting" and "another drain."

- Joyce made the choice to interpret the superficial niceties in their marriage as "everything being okay," and believed there was "no problem" even though Fred had an inherently stressful and demanding job.

- Joyce made a choice to "assume" Fred was managing "fine" because he did not talk to her about his work, despite his leaving the house at 6:30 a.m. and many times not returning home until well after 9 p.m. Since "everything was okay in the bedroom," she figured their relationship was "good."

Again, what I believe readers can learn here is that all choices — including those based on assumptions — lead to consequences. Not all of our choices are conscious, but we must take responsibility for our actions in order to move forward. The following case study further illustrates this point.

CASE STUDY — DEE AND PAT

Dee and Pat scheduled a consult to discuss the challenges in their marriage, and I found out right away that both spouses had successful careers. Dee held a corporate executive job that required her to travel considerably. Meanwhile, Pat was a top-tier sales rep for a medical device company and often worked from home. Their two children were in high school, but when the kids were younger, the couple decided that Pat would stay home for several years and Dee would be the primary breadwinner.

Dee's salary was nearly double Pat's at the time I met with them, but Pat made a sizeable income in his own right and was on track to earn a prestigious sales award for the company that would also lead to a sizeable promotion. The new position, however, would require travel and a fair amount of time at the corporate office.

Dee had recently admitted to Pat that she had slept with "a few" men on business trips over the past several years, but claimed those relationships "meant nothing" to her. Simultaneously, Pat had admitted to Dee that he was embroiled in an "emotional affair" with an old girlfriend in another state, and that they had been talking for the past eighteen months. Although they had not seen each other in person, Pat and his ex had shared some intense sexual exchanges via FaceTime.

Dee and Pat were confused when they came to their first session. They assumed they had no choice but to end their marriage. And while I inquired generally about the affairs, I directed the couple to stay focused on what they wanted their marriage to "look like" above all else. I encouraged them to decide whether they felt my consultation was merely a last-ditch effort to repair their marriage, or if they believed they still had a solid foundation of relationship infrastructure.

It was clear to me that the underlying reasons the spouses had strayed from their marriage and become intimate with other people would only lead to the end of their relationship if Dee and Pat were *committed* to ending it — or if they were so deeply wounded from each other's transgressions that they could not move beyond them. In short, to rebuild their marriage, they needed to look toward a future together.

Of course, since Dee and Pat had both engaged in extracurricular activities with other people for a considerable time, it was unreasonable to think that they would immediately regain unfettered trust for each other. This is where I will say that time and consistency are the two factors that strengthen trust. Over time, when Dee and Pat were monogamous to their marriage both emotionally and physically, and when they were consistent in their behaviors, they began building a bridge in their relationship.

What did this process entail? Over the course of several months, I encouraged Dee and Pat to shift their focus from the past to the future. Dee took a lower-paying job that involved less travel, and Pat agreed to be more transparent about his social media activity — he even blocked the old girlfriend on Facebook and Twitter. Eventually, Pat and Dee began having their own "sexting" sessions when Dee was away. They improved their communication and began opening up when they felt things weren't going well. Although these actions may appear small and superficial, when couples repeat them over time they help to build trust and commitment.

This is why it is so important to overcome bitterness if you decide to repair your relationship. Bitterness results from refusing to forgive the person you consider responsible for your pain. And just as lack of communication is a central cause of divorce in longstanding marriages, improved communication can help spouses push past bitterness and understand each other. Before we close this chapter, I'd like to emphasize that the strongest, most longstanding relationships have one thing in common: a willingness to share and acknowledge different viewpoints in a respectful environment. Dee and Pat achieved this, and so can you.

KEY TAKEAWAYS

- While most relationships start out happy and secure, there is no guide on how to sustain a healthy marriage. Like in business, the key to success lies in the work you do.

- We must take responsibility for our actions in order to make progress. Affairs do not simply "happen," and it's important to recognize that we must change our behaviors in order to improve our relationships.

- Successful marriages require that both partners find some common ground. Resentment accumulates over time, and building healthy communication habits can counter the effects of bitterness.

NEXT UP

In the following chapter, I will detail how couples can build healthy habits and weigh the benefits of their relationship. This begins with each spouse defining what they value, and then evaluating what they are giving up as a result of their decisions. My hope is that spouses will learn to navigate the opportunity costs of their marriage by adopting a business-focused mindset at home.

3 OPPORTUNITY COSTS — EVALUATE YOUR OPTIONS

Failure is simply the opportunity to begin again, this time more intelligently.

—Henry Ford

We have 168 hours each week to devote to activities of import. These activities correlate with what we value. True, not all of us have the same number of "free" hours in a day, but we all make different decisions about how we spend our time and money resources. One determining factor for our choice points is opportunity cost.

In brief, opportunity cost details how to make the best decisions possible, and indicates why people make the choices they do. The principle involves any decision featuring a tradeoff between two or more alternatives. Accordingly, it is expressed as the relative "cost" of one choice compared to the next-best option.[19] [20] [21]

- Opportunity cost is a key concept in economics, expressing "the basic relationship between scarcity and choice."[22] The notion of opportunity cost plays a crucial role in ensuring scarce resources are used efficiently.[23] As such, the concept is not restricted to financial matters, for the costs of lost time, pleasure, or output — or any other benefit that offers utility — are also considered opportunity costs.

Consider the following examples:

---

19 Sikora, M. (2000). *Trying to recoup the cost of lost opportunities. Mergers and Acquisitions, 35(3),* 12–15.

20 Zimmerman, J. L., & Yahya-Zadeh, M. (2011). *Accounting for decision making and control. Issues in Accounting Education, 26(1),* 258-259.

21 Ucbasaran, D., Shepherd, D. A., Lockett, A., & Lyon, S. J. (2013). *Life after business failure: The process and consequences of business failure for entrepreneurs. Journal of Management, 39(1),* 163-202.

22 Durlauf, S. N., & Blume, L. (Eds.). (2008). *New Palgrave dictionary of economics. Basingstoke: Palgrave Macmillan.*

23 Palmer, S., & Raftery, J. (1999). *Economics notes: Opportunity cost. BMJ: British Medical Journal, 318(7197),* 1551.

- If a company spends $250 million on product development, then that is $250 million the company cannot spend on reducing corporate budget deficits, increasing their 401K match, or improving employee health benefits.

- If the government builds a new road, for instance, then that money cannot be spent on matters such as education and health care.

- Time is a major opportunity cost. If you have twelve hours at your disposal during the day, you could spend these hours at work or in leisure. The opportunity cost of spending your day binge-watching Netflix is your inability to complete a project.

Every time you make a decision, there is a certain value you place on that choice. You might not think about it, but every decision has value to you. When you choose one thing over another, you're telling yourself that you value that item more than the other options available to you.

For example, the executive who *consistently* chooses the golf course over family time on weekends is communicating that they value golf more than their personal relationships. I am not speaking against golf, hobbies, or doing activities you like; rather, I am advocating that people consider the costs and benefits of their decision-making.

The opportunity cost of any choice you make is that which you give up as a result of your decision.[24] For example, if you must

---

24 Durlauf, S. N., & Blume, L. (Eds.). (2008). New Palgrave dictionary of economics. Basingstoke: Palgrave Macmillan.

decide between an apple and an orange, and you choose the apple, then your opportunity cost is the orange you could have chosen but didn't. By choosing the apple, you gave up the opportunity to take the orange. The opportunity cost is the value of the opportunity lost.

People incur opportunity costs with every decision they make. However, we often overlook the opportunity costs in our relationships. When you decided to read this book, you gave up other uses of your time. You may have given up a few minutes of your favorite television program, or perhaps a phone call; you may have even forgone the opportunity to spend time with your spouse or children. All costs should be considered when making decisions, not only those that are measured in dollars or rates of return. Even though they do not appear on a balance sheet or income statement, opportunity costs are real in our relationships. By choosing between two courses of action in your marriage, you assume the cost of the option not taken.

CASE STUDY — EDWARDO AND TABITHA

Edwardo was recently appointed Chief Medical Officer at a major hospital in a large metropolitan area. Tabitha, his wife, was a Harvard alumna on track to make partner at a Big 4 accounting firm. When she gave birth to their second child, they agreed that Tabitha would quit her job.

After receiving the promotion, Edwardo began coming home increasingly late. He claimed to be spending long hours in the operating room, and Tabitha assumed this was part of her husband's new role at the hospital. In actuality, Edwardo had started going out for drinks with the other operating room physicians. A female anesthesiologist had taken notice of him, and the two had been having an emotional affair for six months. She and Edwardo talked about the cases they worked on together, the operating room culture, and all the new ways to improve medical processes and procedures; they discussed why they went into medicine and couldn't believe how much they had in common. These exchanges occurred at the end of the day when Edwardo would have otherwise been home with Tabitha.

Edwardo had convinced himself that his colleague "understood him" more than his spouse. He believed that with her, he didn't "have to explain himself" like he did at home. Correspondingly, Tabitha had begun to notice that Edwardo no longer slept in their bed. Citing that he did not want to "wake her up" when he came home late, he had begun sleeping on the couch.

Edwardo came home one day and declared to Tabitha, "I don't love you. I wonder if I ever did — we have nothing in common and I want a divorce." Tabitha was blindsided.

Their pastor, however, suggested that they seek consultation. When they arrived at their appointment, Edwardo had already begun "soul searching" and realized the emotional affair was in part a result of the operating room culture. His colleagues supported his emotional banter with the anesthesiologist, and scheduling nurses made a point of putting the two physicians on cases where they would work together. To address this, Edwardo requested that he and the anesthesiologist work cases on opposite shifts; he also sought out a group within their church to better recognize the error of his judgment.

He recognized that his wife's insecurity about her weight since the birth of their child was a considerable "turn-off," and that he found the female physician's confidence appealing. Awareness was a major step in repairing the marriage.

Unfortunately, Tabitha struggled to move past Edwardo's statement that he "didn't love her and wondered if he ever did," which heightened her insecurities and made her doubt Edwardo's claims that he was in fact in love with her. At the end of our consultation, it became clear that Tabitha needed to make a decision. She could choose to continue resenting Edwardo's behavior, or she could allow herself to be vulnerable again and make reparations.

OPPORTUNITY COSTS AND THE INTERNET

The decisions we make — and the actions we take — affect us a great deal. In this way, the Internet is a dangerous and tricky diversion. Have you ever planned to look something up for just a few minutes, only to realize that two hours have passed? While the extra time you spent online was probably unintentional, and the result of a lack of mindfulness, there are costs to this decision nonetheless. If you tuned in more to your environment, perhaps the cost of your browsing the web would have been a reasonable twenty minutes. Awareness can help reduce the costs in our relationships, and ensure our decisions align with our values to the greatest extent possible.

The impact of spending too much time online can trickle down into your marriage. In 2012, Divorce-Online UK surveyed British divorce lawyers to determine whether there was an anecdotal connection between social media use and divorce. According to that survey, approximately one in three divorces resulted from disagreements relating to social media. Similarly, a 2010 survey by the American Academy of Matrimonial Lawyers (AAML) found that four out of five lawyers used evidence derived from social networking sites in divorce cases, with evidence from Facebook posts being a primary source.[25]

Facebook is a considerable distraction. And while the platform connects us with others, some spouses use it as a diversion when things are not great in their relationship. In this way, Facebook can inadvertently result in marital disconnect.

Of course, all marriages are full of ups and downs. The important thing is how we manage these ebbs and flows. Logging on to Facebook and reconnecting with an old flame under the guise of wanting to "see how they are doing" is not the answer. Reconnecting with someone in your life from a time when you were thinner, younger, and more virile will in most cases take you right to fantasyland.

If you are experiencing troubles in your marriage, focus on your relationship with your spouse. The cost of lost opportunity with your spouse is considerable, and distracting yourself by reconnecting with others on Facebook is not the answer — even if it is under the premise of "friendship."

It is infinitely easier to list what you believe to be "wrong" with your partner than to think about what is right. If you go looking for what is *not* right, you will find it. If you are looking for someone from your past to reaffirm you are still great and worthwhile — to support your theory that your mate finds you subpar — then you are setting up a scenario where this third party will appear wonderful and your spouse will seem dreadful.

---

25 Valenzuela, S., Halpern, D., & Katz, J. E. (2014). *Social network sites, marriage well-being and divorce: Survey and state-level evidence from the United States. Computers in Human Behavior, 36, 94-101.*

Similarly, if you are simply looking for others to reaffirm that *they* would never neglect you or take you for granted like your spouse, you aren't truly giving your relationship a chance. Even if you convince yourself that Jack or Jill appreciates you more than your spouse, focusing your efforts on them is not the answer. Perhaps you simply want to share a tidbit from your day, or maybe you want to reminisce about your glory days in college.

And then, when this person comes to town for a business meeting, maybe you only intend to meet them for coffee. And then coffee turns into lunch, and lunch turns into an afternoon rendezvous or an overnight visit. Suddenly, you have convinced yourself that you value this person more than you value your relationship with your spouse. Granted, your time with this man or woman from your past — the filet mignon and 1,000-count Egyptian cotton sheets — is infinitely more appealing than your daily life. With this person in your thoughts, you forget about the cat puke on the floor. You no longer care about stepping on little Johnny's Legos in the middle of the night, taking your turn with the carpool, managing the knots in your daughter's long hair, or picking up a carton of milk on your way home. You stop thinking about the leftover meatloaf you have already served three times this week, because you are focusing your time and energy on something — or someone — new.

But what are the opportunity costs of this fixation? Imagine what could have happened if you'd focused all this time and energy on your marriage instead. Just think of the connection you could have cultivated with your spouse. Keep these opportunity costs in mind.

SPOTLIGHT ON PORNOGRAPHY

Then there is pornography. Some couples seek consultation to work through their marital issues after one spouse has become reliant on pornography. Initially, both couples consented to the pornography to "spice things up" in the bedroom, but at some point it crossed a line and one partner began to worry about the frequency of use.

In this situation, the other spouse has a choice — to either continue using pornography (with or without their partner's knowledge), or stop using it as a source of stimulation.

Most couples arrive in my office when one spouse claims they will stop using pornography, and the other discovers that their trusted partner has gone behind their back. The spouse feels betrayed by a pattern of lies and deception. The question they tend to ask is, "If you lied to me about the porn, what else have you lied to me about?"

In short, what started as a seemingly innocent way to grow more intimate led to an unexpected outcome. And yet again, the time one or both spouses spent looking at pornography could have been put to better use on intimate pursuits within the marriage.

CASE STUDY — JULIET AND JACQUE

Jacque and Juliet were sexually precocious when they married. This was fine until they had children at the end of a passionate two-year honeymoon period. One day, Jacque left inappropriate images on the computer screen while their son was playing with Hot Wheels on his lap. This freaked Juliet out, but Jacque didn't understand why (which, of course, freaked Juliet out even more).

The incident resulted in some serious arguments — a first in their relationship — and Jacque became depressed. He sought relief in one-night stands. Eventually, Juliet caught her husband having a sexual exploit on FaceTime with a prostitute in the middle of the day, and that was the pivotal event that prompted them to come for help.

Jacque agreed to get rid of all the porn in the house upon Juliet's request, but continued to view it in secret. Their marriage became rockier for a number of reasons: a layoff from Jacque's executive manufacturing operations role when his company merged with another, unresolved family of origin issues, financial struggles, trouble with the in-laws, sick kids, a car accident, and finally Jacque landing a new position as COO at a large national building company. Jacque's ego had also taken a beating during his recent job search, which exacerbated the couple's stress.

Throughout these difficult times, Jacque sought out other women. He began by discussing his explicit fantasies, and gradually took these situations further without telling Juliet. The discovery of his affairs compromised her trust in him, not to mention her own judgment of just about everything that mattered.

Juliet had a difficult time believing that Jacque would end the affairs, as he couldn't give a full account of what he did with the other women. He would lie so convincingly that she believed him until later she exposed his deceit with concrete evidence. Jacque tried to make excuses, but when he couldn't give a full account of his actions, he invented stories to appease his wife.

This kind of secrecy is far from uncommon, as many spouses hide certain behaviors in a misguided effort to put their partner at ease.

Statistics show that pornography is a critical example of a behavior one spouse may want to hide from the other.

In a 2004 testimony before the United States Senate, Dr. Jill Manning shared some interesting data regarding pornography and relationships. In her research, she found that 56 percent of divorce cases involved one party having an obsessive interest in pornographic websites.[26] Specifically, excessive interest in online pornography contributed to more than half of the divorces the attorneys filed in court.[27]

If these numbers are accurate, the implications are profound. Every year for the past decade, there have been roughly 1 million divorces in the United States. If half of these people identify pornography as the culprit, that means there are 500,000 marriages failing — at least in part — due to pornography each year. Indeed, there is usually a plethora of other issues in these marriages, and pornography is merely one symptom of a greater root cause. Nevertheless, the time one or both spouses spend using pornography is tantamount to the golf course example. You have 168 hours each week, so what are you spending this time on? The way we choose to spend these hours has a considerable impact on the outcome of our relationships and overall family health.

---

26 Manning, J. C. (2006). *The impact of Internet pornography on marriage and the family: A review of the research. Sexual Addiction & Compulsivity,* 13(2–3), 131–165.

27 Dedmon, J. (2002, November 14). *Is the Internet bad for your marriage? Online affairs, pornographic sites playing greater role in divorces. Press Release from the Dilenschneider Group, Inc.*

THE ART OF BALANCE

One CEO who has been married twice was depressed and despondent because he "didn't feel on the top of his game" at work. Upon greater exploration, he expressed a deep sense of loss in his past decisions: "I can't remember my kids growing up. I can't remember them when they were young." This CEO had approached his career with the idea that he had to choose between his family and his work, and that it was really impossible to have both.

He recollects: "I believe I could have been a much more effective leader if I had leaned in at home. As my relationship with my family deteriorated, so did my concentration at work, since I was constantly trying to manage it in fits and starts."

How do some succeed in finding "work-life balance"? What techniques have they discovered that so many others seek?

It comes down to choice — evaluating opportunities, building bridges, and emotionally investing in your spouse rather than a third party. You *can* thrive at work and in your personal life, but this requires an investment of the same energy in your marriage and family that you put in your profession. You can engage in a hobby or spend time with your family. You can spend an hour on Netflix, immersed in a video game, browsing Facebook, or watching porn — or you can engage with your spouse and family. All are choice points that have consequences.

As a result, I am urging you to take a hard look at the costs and benefits of your behavior. Take responsibility for your choices, evaluate the opportunity costs of your decisions, and join forces with your spouse to start building a stronger bridge.

KEY TAKEAWAYS

- Opportunity cost is the value of opportunity lost. The opportunity costs of the choices you make are the things you give up as a result of your decisions.

- It is easy to think about what you find "wrong" with your partner, but the best results come when you consider all that is right. If you go looking for what is *not* right, you will find it.

- Spouses can put the same effort into their marriage that they put in at work. A sense of balance will yield optimal results.

NEXT UP

If you and your partner can take a good, hard look at your individual roles in the marriage, then you have already made a significant step in laying the foundation for healthy communication. The next step is to conduct "relationship gap analysis" — another corporate technique involving the comparison of your actual performance to your potential performance — and transform your wish for a solid marriage into a viable plan.

PART 2

THE DECISION

PLANNING FOR A BETTER FUTURE

4 MAKE YOUR WISH A PLAN

Desire is the starting point of all achievement, not a hope, not a wish, but a keen pulsating desire which transcends everything.

—Napoleon Hill

As a highly successful executive, your performance is best while in a certain framework using specific language. To optimize your feelings of comfort, control, and possibility, let's examine the framework and language you use at the office, and apply these elements to your marriage and family situation.

Let's begin by exploring the concept of managerial problems, which involve a gap between the company's current state of affairs and executives' future desired state. In this scenario, problem-solving efforts involve a detailed analysis of the situation and the development of a solution to bridge the gap. While different diagnostic techniques are appropriate in different situations, problem-solving as a formal analytical framework applies to most managerial problems.

This framework is also analogous with the scientific method used in chemistry, astronomy, and other disciplines. In both the sciences and in business, the purpose of the analytic process is to minimize personal bias, promote accuracy, and facilitate communication among all affected parties.

In business, executives need to define "success" in their strategic planning process. They must examine what success equates to, how to measure it, and what indicators — revenue or HR turnover are just two examples — determine the company's success.

Meanwhile, gap analysis details the difference between a company's actual performance and their potential performance.[28] This involves an evaluation of the organization's current state and executives' desired state, followed by the development of a comprehensive plan. This analysis yields a number of insights into the organization's performance and overall functioning.

Only then, by breaking the situation down into a series of easy-to-follow steps, can executives begin to work toward achieving

---

28 *Owusu, G., O'Brien, P., & Shakya, S. (2013). The role of service quality in transforming operations. In Transforming Field and Service Operations (pp. 153–165). Berlin: Springer.*

their corporate goals. The same approach can be very effective in marriage and family relationships.

Gap Analysis

Corporate performance

Where we aim to be

GAP

Where we will end up if we do nothing

Time

Relationship Gap Analysis: Rather than looking at revenue, couples and families must articulate how they perceive success in relation to where they are now. How can the marriage or family environment improve? Where are you compared to where you want to be? Once you establish the steps you must take to achieve success, you can begin to make changes and work toward your end goal. Throughout this process, keep in mind that a goal without a plan is merely a wish.

The following steps are designed to put you on the path to success:

1. ANALYZE YOUR CURRENT SITUATION.

It is infinitely easier to identify what is wrong with your marriage or family dynamic than it is to simply assess the situation. As mentioned earlier, you must not forget to acknowledge what is *right*. Once you delve into the good, you will have a solid foundation from which to build. This is very similar to strategic planning where a company must examine where it is in the business landscape presently to set feasible goals for the future.

Many couples come to my office with a resident laundry list of grievances. When I ask them to address what is working in their

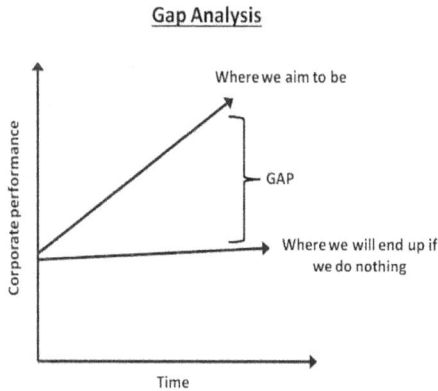

relationship, it changes the dynamic and overall trajectory of our conversation. Suddenly, the relationship is still alive and thriving, and the couple realizes there are steps they can take to strengthen their bond down the road. Again, this is equally relevant to volatile family relationships. It is much easier to see the bad in things, but we cannot forget to discuss the good. Note that pessimism dissolves relationships quickly, while optimism helps to strengthen them.

In my practice, I usually ask couples to list several qualities they appreciate in each other. Since negative traits are more readily re-called, it is important that both parties take the time to step back and name what is right and good. In doing so, they can focus on the positive attributes of their marriage, and they will be more fo-cused on growing together. Family members — siblings, parents, and anyone else in the unit — can employ the same strategy.

A word of caution: I am not implying that you ignore the chal-lenges in your relationships. Addressing the negative is certainly of merit. However, you must examine the situation objectively without overlooking the positive aspects of your marriage or family environment. If your current situation is all negative, and there are no positive attributes, then you will be less invested in improving your dynamic and strengthening your bond.

In short, you will be more inclined to step up and work on your mar-riage if you reflect on the good. Moreover, to strategize solutions and ultimately reach your goals, you must have a realistic take on what is happening right now. Families can do the same, including children who have turbulent relationships with their parents. The difficulties will be addressed in time, but you must believe your relationships are worth fighting for in order to make any lasting changes.

2. IDENTIFY YOUR DESIRED FUTURE STATE.

The next step is to articulate what you want your family dynamic to look like. It is not enough to say you want to be happy, argue less, or communicate better. These goals, however laudable, are not very specific. They leave considerable room for question due to their subjectivity. How can you possibly determine when you arrive at your desired future state without any concrete milestones or a definitive end goal? If a couple decides to work toward communicating more effectively, how can they possibly measure what constitutes "effective" communication? When the future state is vague, tracking one's progress becomes an impossible feat.

As homework after an initial consult, I often ask each person to come up with a list or description of what they would expect the relationship to "look like" if it were successful. If you have a tangible end goal, then it will be much easier to map your course and reach your destination. Correspondingly, once all parties are clear on what they desire for the future, they can articulate their needs in a detailed fashion in pursuit of where they "want to be."

This is not unlike a corporate action plan, where we must detail our objectives before mapping out the relevant action steps. Well-formed objectives are achieved through clear action steps that cascade into a plan of *how* we're going to achieve *what* we listed in the strategic plan.

Here are eight things we need to consider to ensure a solid action plan:

1. Ownership

One person must be responsible for tracking progress toward each objective, keeping the team informed, ensuring timely action steps, and adjusting the actions as we learn what needs to change. Accountability is key.

2. Action Steps

Action steps lay out a clear path on how each objective should be achieved. If the objective is the *what*, then the action steps are the *how*. It's critical that the action steps are clear, actionable concepts rather than vague ideas.

3. Responsibility

One person must be responsible for leading each action step. This does not need to be the same person in charge of the overall objective. In many cases, several people share responsibility for the various action steps.

4. Support

Those responsible for each action step require support — often from multiple people. The key is that these individuals are acting as a support system in some capacity, and assisting the person responsible in their effort to complete each action step.

5. Communication

It is critically important to keep relevant people in the communication loop for each action step. Make sure these individuals are communicated of any progress that is made, which will allow them to work toward other actions and objectives.

6. Metrics and Budget

Each action step must have a metric that indicates the action is complete. You might need specific resources to execute. For example, if you need to survey your customers and don't have the internal resources to do so, using an external resource will require money that might not be available in your operating budget. Make sure you have the resources to meet your objectives.

7. Milestone Date

The date the action step needs to begin to reach the project's completion date. (In high school and college, for instance, we were all subconsciously programmed that Thursday night was the best time to start writing an essay due Friday morning.)

8. Completion Date

The date by which the action step ought to be completed. This is a straightforward, albeit crucial part of the framework. Keep in mind, however, that all of the abovementioned steps work together to form a cohesive action plan.

From a marital perspective, this process might appear intense and time-consuming. That said, when both spouses work toward achieving the same end goals, they need to agree on what their desired future state will look like — and these steps will help them discuss the elements on which they need to agree.

By failing to acknowledge this framework, conflicting viewpoints risk harming any progress that is made. Conversely, by having a consultant serve as a mediator and at times a translator to decipher what each person is saying, both parties can gain insights into where they are headed.

That said, one of the biggest problems facing companies and other organizations is how to plan for the future. What to invest in? Where to place your bets? We don't have a crystal ball to predict the future, but creative thinking skills and proven behaviors help companies bring powerful future scenarios to fruition. Strategic growth planning is the systematic process in which company leaders determine the way they will progress from their current situation to their desired future state.

The plan identifies growth priorities specific to the organization. Moreover, it generates a strategic growth vision for how the organization wishes to be moving forward. Lastly, the plan establishes a roadmap of actions that are required to transform the organization's current situation into the desired future situation.

And so it is with relationships. Articulate what you want your family dynamic to look like, and then set the course for your action steps. It is not enough to say you will work to be happy, argue less, or communicate better. These goals, however laudable, are not very specific. They're also subjective, which makes it difficult for couples to track their progress.

Objectivity is essential, and it is important to be as detailed as possible as you work toward your desired future state. For instance, rather than saying you want to fight "less often," commit to no longer raising your voice, or pledge to reduce the frequency of your fighting by 50% within two weeks. Think of concrete ways to

bridge the gap, and then start cultivating a more "successful" relationship.

3. DETERMINE WHAT YOU CAN DO TO BRIDGE THE GAP.

After defining your current situation and your desired future state, you can think of concrete ways to bridge the gap and cultivate a "successful" relationship. While identifying the steps to take may seem deceptively easy, this process usually requires a series of complex actions to help truly bridge the gap. In actuality, many situations that bring couples to my office are underlying symptoms of much larger concerns.

A number of couples visit my practice due to frequent arguments about sex, parenting, and money. Specifically, many couples have different views of what constitutes "good" or "frequent" sex. Some of my colleagues mistakenly present a host of solutions for the couple, such as scheduling frequent date nights or booking a vacation to spend more time together. These, however, are merely short-term solutions. And while there are usually substantial concerns at play here, most of these solutions have little to do with sex.

In other words, the underlying cause of this issue might be feeling disconnected from one's spouse, or feeling overwhelmed because one person believes they are doing more around the house. In many cases, a lack of appreciation is at play, and poor communication is another a common issue. Perhaps the couple would be more intimate if they communicated more productively. Families experience very similar challenges in their relationships. Perhaps a working mother is concerned about her daughter's poor performance in school, when in actuality the teen is feeling neglected and acting out to attract her parents' attention. More often than not, the main symptom does not account for why clients come to my office. It is only upon further examination that we can identify the root cause and make changes that will be more enduring to the relationships at play.

So, looking at the gap analysis in your relationships, determine where you are in the moment. Then identify where you hope to be in the future, mapping and analyzing the circumstances surrounding your relationships. Just like in business, all parties should be working toward the same objectives.

KEY TAKEAWAYS

- Relationships should be examined objectively, without overlooking the positive. If you believe your marriage is all negative, then you will be less invested in making improvements.

- Once you define your desired future state, create an action plan to help bridge the gap and cultivate a healthy, thriving relationship. This process requires a series of complex actions that both you and your spouse must take.

- Note that bridging the gap involves adopting a shared perspective, even if you must make compromises in your relationship. At the very least, actively try to understand where your spouse is coming from.

NEXT UP

Your values relate to how you spend your time, both at home and at work. You may think you value your personal relationships, but is this really true? It is to an extent, of course, but it's important to achieve — or at least be aware of — the proper balance based on what you desire in your life. Your behavior can be very telling in whether you prioritize family over work or vice versa; and in the next chapter, we are going to explore how your values affect your marriage and family environment.

5 YOUR CHOICES REFLECT YOUR VALUES

Your beliefs become your thoughts. Your thoughts become your words. Your words become your actions. Your actions become your habits. Your habits become your values. Your values become your destiny.

—Mahatma Gandhi

In our bonds with other people, and in marriage specifically, it is evident that three core principles underlie our decision-making and values. By considering your values from the perspective of these three principles, you can reduce your risk of disconnect and make progress toward relationship alignment.

From there, you can position yourself to make changes so you and your spouse have the opportunity to strengthen your marriage. Ultimately, it is your decision to hold on to the wreckage of your communication and perpetuate the same old cycle of discontentment.

But that's not the only option available to you. You and your spouse can also make a conscious decision to put in the work and move forward in your relationship.

PRINCIPLE 1: VALUES ARE MORE IMPORTANT THAN WORDS.

Everyone lives their life with an internalized value system or moral code, but few people take the time to actively sort out what they really believe in. Because of this disparity, they often feel conflicted when making regular decisions about time, money, and other personal matters.

Let's begin by examining this principle from a business perspective. Jim Collins made a compelling case for the power of core values in his book *Built to Last.* [29]

It is challenging, if not impossible, to accurately create core values for your company if you do not have a clear set of personal values. [30]

Similar to the core values of a company, personal core values guide our behavior and decision-making to propel us toward a desired

---

29 Collins, J. C., & Porras, J. I. (2005). *Built to last: Successful habits of visionary companies.* New York, NY: Random House.

30 Eisenbeiss, S. A., Van Knippenberg, D., & Fahrbach, C. M. (2015). Doing well by doing good? Analyzing the relationship between CEO ethical leadership and firm performance. *Journal of Business Ethics, 128(3),* 635-651.

path. Core values help us manage our personal resources such as time and money, and reinforce the fact that when we change our values we also change our behavior.[31] This principle is further exemplified in the concept of "values-based leadership."[32]

Values-based leadership indicates that an individual's leadership "must be rooted in who you are and what matters most to you... coming down to doing the right thing and doing the best you can." There are four steps to realizing values-based leadership:

1. Self-Reflection
You must determine your values — that is, what you stand for — and reflect on the meaning of what you believe in. Look inward, and consistently work toward improving your self-awareness.

2. Balance
You must strive for objectivity, and examine situations from multiple perspectives to truly understand them. Be willing to learn, and consider all points of view with an open mind.

3. Self-Confidence
You need to accept yourself in order to be a values-based leader. Do not be afraid to defend your beliefs, acknowledge your strengths *and* your weaknesses, and make conscious improvements.

4. Humility
You must also remember who you are. Do not forget where you came from, no matter how successful you become. Be humble, and no matter their background, treat others with respect.

---

31 Frost, J. (2014). *Values based leadership. Industrial and commercial training,* 46(3), 124-129. Sheehan, 2000.

32 Kraemer, H. M. (2011). *From values to action: The four principles of values-based leadership. John Wiley & Sons.*

These four principles apply to all human beings, from executives to married couples and many others. In every role you fill, keep these pillars in mind. Doing so will help you focus on what matters most.

In a corporate setting, for employees to believe in the sincerity and depth of their organizational values, the company leadership team must guide by example and communicate the values to the entire workforce on an ongoing basis. The effectiveness of these values lies in how well they are embodied by the organization.

It is important to note that values apply to so much more than just our work. Our values reflect who we are on a daily basis, in everything we do at home and on the job. This holistic approach is designed to help us take on a leadership role in all aspects of our lives, not just in our careers.

Say one of your espoused values is "My family comes before my job." If, in this case, your employees see you working so many hours that you rarely have time for your family, they will conclude that the real company core value is "My work is more important than my family." Unfortunately, your family will receive the same message. Granted, executives work long hours, but when the CEO goes home for the evening, so does everyone else. Meanwhile, if the CEO is lonely and bored, the team will go out for drinks after work, and the spouses are left at home.

Consider the following values-based relationship decision. A successful nonprofit lawyer and her information architect spouse developed flexible schedules that allowed them to limit their childcare expenses and spend time with their kids before and after school. Both spouses liked that their jobs didn't demand tons of time away from the family. Neither was interested in being promoted at work — even though it might also mean more money, prestige, or new challenges to tackle — because they enjoyed being home with few career responsibilities after hours.

What does this mean for you? As an executive, it is important that you establish not just your own values, but values that represent your company leadership. These should be based on your actions. In simple terms, when your behavior reflects the extent to which you value your family, your actions will trickle down to everyone else within the organization. It is up to you to set a positive example — to set the tone for how you want to see things change at home and at work.

Interestingly, one challenge I have lies in convincing overworked CEOs that investing in personal time will enhance their performance at work. Lack of balance affects our stress tolerance, and ultimately becomes another destabilizer when we need to be composed. This investment is also a much better example of leadership than many portray. When a leader completes their work while maintaining stability and balance in their life, it sets a much better example for others in the company who may be struggling with similar challenges.

If you want to leave a memorable legacy, you must first determine what you believe in — you must define the things that are most important to you. Then, you need to evaluate whether you are living in alignment with those values. After all, your employees, spouse, and children will see your values more clearly in your actions and lifestyle than in your words.

PRINCIPLE 2: YOU DO WHAT YOU VALUE.

The way you conduct yourself and the way you expect your employees to conduct themselves sets a precedent for the company value system. For instance, if you say the company values family life, and yet team members feel the need to stay at the office until 10 p.m. each night, the company values and actions are not in alignment. This can lead to resentment, frustration, and confusion for your staff and family members.

As stated earlier, we only have so much time, energy, and emotional resources each day. Therefore, the way we choose to spend these resources is a direct reflection of our value system. Whether you acknowledge this consciously or unconsciously, our activities are a clear indication of our value system.

So take what you believe to be your personal and family values, and operationalize them into your behaviors. When you weigh the responsibilities of family, community, and business, you have to make choices and define your priorities in order to act based on any sort of value system. In short, your values must reflect your actions.

What does this mean for you? For example, if you claim to value your spouse, their feelings, and the longevity of your marriage, then you will make conscious decisions to avoid being self-centered or personally entitled.[33] This, in turn, will make you much less likely to consider divorce as a viable option when you experience turbulence in your marriage. Married couples, both indi-

---

33 Doherty, W. J. (2013). *Take back your marriage: Sticking together in a world that pulls us apart.* New York, NY: Guilford Press.

vidually and mutually, must take responsibility for changing their actions to reflect their values.[34]

If you say you value time with your family, but choose to focus on distractors such as work, volunteerism, and the Internet, then your actions do not support your assertion that you value family time. If, upon taking a closer look, you feel your actions do not reflect your values, you must change your behaviors — limit your Internet use, cut back on all those late nights at the office, and volunteer at times when your spouse and children are busy with other tasks. It sounds simple, but making the decision to change can be quite difficult.

Note that in most cases, our values and behaviors fall out of alignment over time. At the beginning of a marriage, when spouses feel as though they have nothing but each other, they focus intently on the building blocks of a healthy marriage. However, as the relationship moves forward, career obligations and material items begin to accumulate and distract us from the essentials needed for a successful marriage. At this point, our actions and main areas of focus seem to shift — we start to worry more about the appraisal value of our home than the value of our marriage and family relationships. Or perhaps we check the health of our retirement account more often than we assess the health of our marriage. Maybe we spend more time looking after the car than the person beside us in bed.

CASE STUDY — BILL AND SAMANTHA

Bill and Samantha were in their mid-forties with a two-year-old daughter when they sought help for their deteriorating marriage. Both were successful executives: Samantha was Chief of Surgery

---

34 *Ibid.*

at a university-based medical center, while Bill was a partner at a large accounting firm.

Both spouses claimed they felt successful at work and yet highly distressed at home, where tension and frequent fighting kept them angry, unhappy, and contemplating divorce. Samantha indicated that she always felt dismissed, especially when she was upset about something. Bill added, "Our communication is not good at all. We argue a lot. Please give us the tools to communicate and make our relationship better."

Digging in further, the couple appeared to have different perceptions of what a healthy marriage entailed. Bill was often in a mode of "all about me" — a lifestyle of occupying himself with work and recreational activities such as mountain biking, running, and swimming. He functioned like a bachelor, with minimal involvement in his family life. He had a habitual pattern of non-listening, brushing Samantha off when they tried to discuss issues that concerned her, which typically triggered the couple's arguments. Their frequent fighting further discouraged Bill from spending time at home. While he might not have been aware of it, being with his family exhausted him. Bill felt there were too many demands on him.

As things begin to accumulate in our homes and lives, they demand our money, energy, and time. As a result, we have few resources left over to keep our marriage healthy and thriving. Granted, a nice home, a luxury car, and a full retirement account are nothing to be ashamed of, but they do not in themselves constitute a successful marriage. In fact, I have found the most successful couples invest their money, energy, and time into their marriage, as a means of combining personal commitment with intentional focus on growing together. (This is one way in which Bill and

Samantha's relationship fell short.) In the retreats I facilitate for executive couples, the investment proves well worth both spouses' time and money. Spending time together in an open, peaceful environment promotes clear thinking, which can help you improve your value system.

MARITAL INVESTMENTS

Most wealthy people have a sound investment strategy. People who succeed with their investments understand the long-term view and make commitments accordingly. One method to succeed in the stock market is called dollar-cost averaging, or DCA. With DCA, you figure out how much you're going to invest in the market, and invest that amount regularly — regardless of whether the market is up or down. *You invest no matter what.* This is a long-term plan that keeps you from exiting the market during difficult times.

What does DCA look like in marriage? Only you know the best investments for your relationship. That said, the following are two of the most powerful investments one can make in *any* relationship:

Disconnect to Connect. Many executives believe their work life is far more important than their home life. This is a toxic mindset. Oftentimes, the shock of the executive's marriage nearly falling apart will inspire them to pay more attention to their spouse. In many cases, however, they will only go through the motions of putting family over work. Actually following through is essential in this way.

True change comes from being mentally present at home. This requires disconnecting from work, turning off your cell phone, and focusing entirely on your family. Cook with your spouse, or help the kids with their homework — these are great places to start.

My clients often accuse their spouses of being physically present, but mentally absent. If you find yourself sneaking into the bathroom to write a work email, then you're not in the moment with your family. Step away from the C-suite pressure cooker from time to time, and work to change your perspective.

Participate and Communicate. To sustain a healthy marriage, both spouses need to materially participate in their family life. Even the busiest CEOs ought to drive a carpool, make peanut-butter sandwiches, and attend school events. You cannot outsource being there for your family.

Being there, of course, requires sound communication and prioritization. By the time some couples reach my office, they'll have gone days without communicating. Being completely "tuned in" to your family is critical. Prioritize your weekly date night, and recognize the value of the special time you spend with your kids. Add "family" appointments to your calendar to avoid double-booking yourself — and do *not* cancel them.

If you don't carve out time for your family, you won't make the investments you need to promote a healthy marriage. Thriving couples proactively invest in each other.

UNDERLYING MOTIVATION

What separates the 10 percent of executives who succeed both at home and at work from those who have successful careers but marital or family problems? The theme — and I may sound like a broken record at this point — is choice. It's a matter of organizing around our priorities in order to nurture all the aspects of our lives that we value. While this may sound simple, in actuality *choosing* to value the things we consider most important can be quite difficult to operationalize. For many, this is a longstanding issue.

How can it be this complicated? In my experience, couples have struggled with changing their actions because doing so involves making a choice not once, but every single day. These choices also reflect our motivations (i.e., how our motivations manifest in our behaviors). Executives must ask themselves why they do what they do, and explore where their motivational drive is centered. Looking inward will likely prove a challenge if you find your values are not in alignment with your behaviors.

By way of illustration, few would say they are not motivated in their career, at least to some degree, by monetary compensation. This motivation is not inherently negative, but it can lead to the frequent purchase of items that demonstrate status or power. Do you ever find yourself buying and showcasing vehicles and other toys that will publicly demonstrate your prosperity? And if so, does this align with your value system? Think about this — about whether your actions are indicative of the person you truly want to be.

The alternative to this involves taking your financial, time-based, and emotional resources, and devoting them to pursuits that will nurture your marriage and family. True, one can have it both ways — you can have a nice car, a ski chalet in the mountains, and still spend a great deal of quality time with your family — but you must be aware of the motivations behind the actions you take.

Eleanor Roosevelt summarized this point quite eloquently:

One's philosophy is not best expressed in words; it is expressed in the choices one makes. In the long run, we shape our lives and we shape ourselves. The process never ends until we die. And, the choices we make are ultimately our own responsibility.

CASE STUDY — LINDA AND BOB

I would like to offer further insights into the importance of upholding a strong value system. To do so, I will share my experiences with Bob and Linda, a couple who came to see me in order to strengthen their marriage. From their first visit, it became clear to me that the spouses had very different values.

Bob was the lead mechanic at a high-end auto dealership, where he worked on imported cars. He had a limited education and admittedly felt inferior because of this. Moreover, since Bob had grown up in poverty, he told me he wanted more for his family than what he'd had in his youth. He was good with his hands and mechanically inclined. He was liked by his customers, and sought after for his dedication and skill as a mechanic.

And yet, despite his day job offering a perfectly adequate salary, especially when coupled with his wife's own income, he wanted more. He would have preferred that Linda not have to work, and Bob dreamed of having more time with his family.

To bring his vision of being a business owner to fruition, and with Linda's emotional and financial support, Bob started a new shop at home. He became increasingly busy as a result, to the point where he was working his day job with imported cars an hour from their residence, and then coming home at night and working some more until it was time to go to sleep. As his home shop started to grow, Bob developed a loyal following, and people started traveling a considerable distance to have him work on their vintage imported cars.

After about eight months of working two jobs, Bob's impossibly busy schedule led him and Linda to a marital consultation. Linda's complaint was that Bob was no longer available for her and the kids. She claimed that even when he was physically present at home, he was thinking about the shop; his focus was entirely on what he could do next with the business. Linda needed Bob to help their three children with homework, evening chores, and other family activities. Bob, however, simply didn't have the time, and after dinner each night he would immediately retreat to his home shop to work on more cars.

During appointments Bob would say all the right things. He agreed to be more available, and stated he would limit his work at home until the kids were in bed. In addition, he said he would help around the house and be more emotionally available for his wife. Each time I met with them, Bob and Linda would leave the session feeling hopeful. And then, two or three weeks later, they would come to another session, at which time Linda would say that Bob had made changes for five or six days, only to fall back into old habits by the end of the week.

Bob would respond, "Just a while longer, and then I can leave my day job as a mechanic and do the home shop full-time." But he never said when enough would truly be enough. Would Bob ever feel his home business was secure?

Linda didn't know, and frankly, neither did Bob. Previously, Bob had said he was working to make money for his family, so they could enjoy nicer toys, jet skis, vacations, and so on. This was why he worked so much, or so Bob said.

But the issues in their marriage weren't limited to the number of hours Bob worked. Bob had also started to drink more frequently, particularly on weekends, and he took up marijuana to cope with the stress of his two jobs. His actions did not reflect the values he claimed to have, and it became clear to me that he had fallen into a trap of his own making.

Looking deeply into Bob, I discovered he was emotionally barren and depressed — it took all the energy he had to put on a good face. In private, he still struggled to process the fact that his broken relationships with friends and family members — and ultimately the downfall of his marriage with Linda — were a direct result of his choices. He had been so driven by the artificial signifiers of career success that he failed to see how important it was to find success in his relationships. In the end, Bob neglected his spouse and children, his health, and other important aspects of his life in a superficial quest for success and "freedom" that he felt only money would allow him to enjoy. While Bob's idea of being connected to his family was laudable, the choices he made to accomplish this goal were off-base.

Again, as stated in principles 1 and 2, values are more than words because we do what we value most. Bob was doing what he valued by working around the clock, and through his actions it became clear he did not value his marriage as much as he claimed. He chose to focus exclusively on his work, and as a result, he did not succeed in his marriage.

EMS and relationship consultations are only effective if you follow through with what you agree to work on, and take action for a sustained time period to make positive changes in your life. Talking a good game, saying the right things during appointments with a third party, and then doing nothing does not yield sustained marital progress.

OPERANT CONDITIONING AND INTERMITTENT REINFORCEMENT

Retailers have established a plethora of marketing and business development strategies to understand the triggers that compel people to spend money. Slot machines, for instance, rely on the effect of variable interval operant conditioning. In simple terms, slot machines rarely "pay out" — but when they do, the rewards are often substantial. This prompts people to gamble more frequently in hopes of a generous payout.

Operant conditioning indicates that if every time you behave in a certain way you receive a certain response, you'll receive reinforcement that will subsequently modify the original behavior. Reinforcement can be positive or negative, and either increase or decrease the target behaviors.

The same can be said of married couples intermittently showing the behavior each spouse yearns for in the other. As soon as one spouse sees what they want so desperately from their partner, even if only for a couple of days, they will think, *I know they are capable of doing X, so maybe if Y or Z happens, my spouse will go back to being the person I fell in love with.*

Let's return to Bob and Linda for a moment. Our time together ended with my confronting Bob, as no amount of cognitive restructuring (AKA "thinking differently") was going to change this marriage. It truly came down to choice. If Bob continued to choose work and marijuana to combat his self-induced stress, then he would lose his family to divorce.

Of course, Linda did not want her marriage to end, but she recognized that she could only control herself and her own actions. Her wishing, hoping, and pleading with Bob to change was of little use because nobody was going to force Bob to change other than himself, and ultimatums are not effective communication tools. Linda recognized that her husband needed to decide whether the loss of his family outweighed the gain he would get from the work and lifestyle choices he was making (including the excessive alcohol consumption and marijuana).

Linda came back for an individual session about six weeks later. She confessed that Bob had gone through another cycle of their usual pattern — things got better for a week, and then the workaholic behaviors and substance abuse issues picked up again as soon as Bob's stress increased.

If nothing changes, nothing changes. We can decide to change ourselves, but we cannot make that decision for other people.

This brings me back to the second phase of the relationship gap analysis from the previous chapter — the importance of identifying our desired future state. To improve the health of your marriage, you must think about what you want your marriage and family to look like. You cannot very well achieve your goals if you haven't yet defined them. Accordingly, you must think about your destination before you begin your journey. If you want to drive somewhere but have no idea where you are going, then how can you possibly navigate the best route?

The way you decide to reach your desired destination is much more than a theoretical exercise. It requires self-reflection and the ability to take personal responsibility for the choices you have made — specifically those choices leading up to the current state of your marriage and family relationships. Then, you must commit to change the behaviors that contributed to your relationship troubles. Think about why you picked up this book in the first place, and strive to change your actions so they align with your values.

Unfortunately for Linda and Bob, Bob did not reflect on his value system and take the personal initiative to change their marriage. Fortunately for you, though, you can learn from Bob's mistakes and put in the time and effort required to help make your marriage a success. The decision is yours.

PRINCIPLE 3: SET YOUR PRIORITIES.

One of the most interesting things I have learned in the corporate world? Many of the elements that create a successful home life are equally effective in building a successful career. These elements include setting priorities, fostering an atmosphere of open communication, establishing a cohesive relationship with other executives, setting high standards and working hard to meet those standards. As an executive, you already have these tools in your arsenal, and you have a great deal of experience using these tools to achieve fabulous results. Now it's a matter of applying these tools to your home life.

Priority setting is a collaborative effort. If you consider a certain priority a major value, but your spouse does not (i.e., bringing flowers at the cost of being on time for a dinner), then you are missing the mark. No matter how hard you try, if your priorities do not line up with those of your beloved, then there will be limited progress in your effort to find balance and unity in your personal life.

But making your personal life a priority requires more than simply acknowledging the division line between work and home. Strong relationships must be built deliberately between you and the members of your family. This is where your values and priorities come into play. If you value your family, you must make time for them. You need to commit the time required to foster the relationships that are most important to you.

To do so, you must determine what exactly is important to you. Not just in the present moment — money and power are fleeting — but decades from now. What epitaph or quote do you want on your gravestone? Would it be an ideal you worked for, an honest representation of yourself, or a kind word to people who grieve for you? No matter what it is, keep in mind that the ways you spend your time and energy are precisely what determine your value system.

I believe that for the vast majority of people, the most important thing we will ever accomplish takes place inside the home. If you're successful in your marriage and family relationships, you'll be better prepared to face not only the challenges of your career, but the challenges of life in general. By all means, do not overlook the importance of strengthening your marriage and family relationships.

KEY TAKEAWAYS

- Your destination is no less important than your journey. Consider what you want your relationship to look like, as you cannot achieve your goals without defining them.

- Your personal values reflect your priorities, just like a company's core values reflect the organization. Keep in mind that when you change your actions, you also change your values.[35]

- Successful couples invest in their marriage. Healthy relationships require careful collaboration and strategic planning, and yet each spouse must commit to grow together. While we can decide to change ourselves, we cannot make that decision for other people, no matter how invested we are in the relationship.

NEXT UP

In the following chapter, I will detail another tool you can use to sift through the symptoms and identify the real cause of the difficulties in your marriage. Again, you will find the only way to solve problems in your relationship is to change your behaviors such that your actions align with your values. You and your partner must make the conscious decision to embody these values.

No matter the method you use to uncover the problem, please note that it is only by truly appreciating your marriage and making choices that reflect how much it means to you that your relationship can change for the better. Focus on your values above all else, and with the right decision-making, the rest will fall into place.

---

35 Frost, J. (2014). *Values based leadership. Industrial and commercial training,* 46(3), 124-129. Sheehan, 2000.

6 UNDERSTAND YOUR SYMPTOMS

If you don't ask the right questions, you don't get the right answers. A question asked in the right way often points to its own answer. Asking questions is the ABC of diagnosis. Only the inquiring mind solves problems.

—Edward Hodnett

Many couples attribute the problems they experience in their relationship to a single cause. For instance, couples often come to me because they believe they need to "communicate better." They land in my office to address issues involving sex, money, time, and parenting — and yet the challenges they face are in fact symptoms of

89

other causes. In relationships, no problem is "black and white." There are inherent gray areas that must be addressed.

In medicine, it's easy to understand the difference between treating symptoms and curing the condition. While a broken wrist hurts a great deal, painkillers will only eliminate the symptoms of the fracture. The patient will still need further treatment to help their bones heal.

Marriage works the same way in that couples must identify the source of their problems in order to truly solve them. As the causes become more specific, so do the solutions. Ultimately, both spouses need to take specific actions in response to the root causes of the issues they face.[36]

ROOT CAUSE ANALYSIS

Root cause analysis (RCA) is a process often used in business. The idea is to identify the "root causes" of problems or certain scenarios, and subsequently develop strategies to address them.[37] Effective management requires not only a quick response to problems, but also a series of proven preventative measures designed to keep things in order.

---

36 Galley, M. (2008). *Basic elements of a comprehensive investigation: Three steps and three tools that organize and improve your problem solving capability. ThinkReliability.* Retrieved from http://www.thinkreliability.com/pdf/root-cause-analysis-article-basic-elements.pdf.

37 Conger, S. (2015). *Six sigma and business process management. In Handbook on Business Process Management 1 (pp. 127-146). Springer, Berlin, Heidelberg.*

In business, RCA identifies the underlying reasons why an incident or situation might have occurred. Similarly, in marriage, we can use RCA to explore the circumstances and habits affecting spouses.[38]

Root cause analysis focuses on three basic questions:

What is the problem?

Why did it happen?

What will be done to prevent it from occurring again, or to change the behavior moving forward? [39] [40]

With RCA, the assumption is that systems and events are interrelated. The above questions illuminate why a circumstance might have occurred. In simple terms, an action in one area triggers an action in another, and the process repeats. By tracing these actions back to their origin, you can discover where the problem began, and how it grew into the symptoms you are currently facing.[41]

PINPOINTING THE PROBLEM

Some say acknowledging the problem is half of the solution, but that may be an understatement. Without admitting to the problems we face, there is little chance for a solution because we tend

---

38 Ketola, J., & Roberts, K. (2003). *Correct!, prevent!, improve!: Driving improvement through problem solving and corrective and preventive action.* Milwaukee, WI: American Society for Quality Press.

39 Heuvel, L. N. V. (2005). *Root cause analysis handbook: a guide to effective incident investigation.* Rothstein Associates Inc.

40 Latino, R. J., Latino, K. C., & Latino, M. A. (2016). *Root cause analysis: improving performance for bottom-line results.* CRC press.

41 Rasiel, E. M., & Friga, P. N. (2002). *The McKinsey mind, understanding and implementing problem-solving tools and management techniques of the world's top strategic consulting firm.* New York, NY: McGraw Hill.

to take a "wait and see" approach. Simply waiting for things to get better is very different from discussing the source of the issue, and strategizing concrete ways to fix it.

There is a stigma attached to marital and family issues in American culture. Bringing up problems may result in a loved one's negative reaction, which some fear will make matters worse. Indeed, minor difficulties can be solved without professional assistance — and there are admittedly reasons why some prefer not to address their problems. In fact, the average troubled couple waits six years before they consider marital consultation, and as a result their problems are usually quite substantial when they decide to take action.[42]

However, this does not have to be the case. Couples who regularly check in with each other can resolve problems quickly, as they are more likely to acknowledge that minor problems are normal. In this regard, families can grow closer by opening new lines of communication and inviting all members to solve the problems that concern them. For this reason, acknowledging the problem is a regular practice that I suggest you and your spouse engage in together, and I encourage you to include your children as well. This process is explained in more detail in the following section.

THE PROBLEM-SOLVING PROCESS

When you and your spouse set aside time, perhaps weekly, to check in with each other, you present the opportunity to discuss any potential problems affecting your marriage. Then, once you define

---

42 Gottman, J., & Silver, N. (2015). *The seven principles for making marriage work: A practical guide from the country's foremost relationship expert.* Easton, PA: Harmony.

a problem, you can seek solutions by using a rational problem-solving process.

Problem-solving in couples is different from your standard math problem, as there is almost always more than one viable solution. In fact, there are typically a number of different solutions that might address the main challenges you are facing. We will explore this in more detail, and examine the best ways to find the root cause of a problem later.

For now, let's focus on the act of problem-solving. Effective problem-solving is an ongoing process that involves more than pure logic and reasoning, and couples must be willing to change some of their behaviors for the health of their relationship. In addition, they must implement various solutions and see what happens before evaluating the results. The process is fairly scientific in nature, and it works best via trial and error. It will not only help couples determine how well a given solution might work, but also whether additional steps are needed.

This is relevant because when working with couples, issues emerge at different times. In most cases, there are multiple solutions required to solve the overarching problem. The first step, though, is to construct a clear definition of the problem. This is often difficult, yet it is a crucial step in working through the root cause of the issue, and addressing head-on the reasons the spouses have come to see me.

The first step is to define the problem. A major difficulty often lies in the way couples initially describe their issues. When couples frame their problems as complaints, they tend to spark a series of denials and counter-complaints[43] that hinder marital harmony. For example, a couple comes in with the husband complaining that he is not "getting enough sex," which is a symptom of a greater problem. Perhaps the wife responds by indicating that she "could take or leave having sex" with him. The main problem, as defined by the husband, is that he does not feel connected with his wife; he may claim she just "doesn't want to have sex" with him. In contrast, the wife feels she is just an object for her husband's orgasmic stress release and that he doesn't make enough of an effort to bring her to climax.

But looking deeper, the root cause of this couple's lack of intimacy has more to do with the wife feeling insecure on an emotional or financial level (perhaps her husband has a history of affairs, or of being a spendthrift). Therefore, she does not want to "give herself" to her husband because he keeps threatening to leave if things do not "get fixed" in the bedroom.

Reiterating concepts at the beginning of this chapter, the presenting issue or main complaint is rarely the real issue the couple is facing. Rather, it is a symptom of the root cause.

Obvious: The symptom, the "leaves" — what one sees above the surface.

Possibly unclear: The trunk, or the actual problem that needs addressing.

---

43 Vuchinich, S. (1999). *Problem solving in families: Research and practice (v.13)*. New York, NY: Sage.

Not Obvious: The underlying causes, the "root"— what lies below the surface.

The illustration below reveals how root cause analysis can be used to dissect cause, problem, and effects.

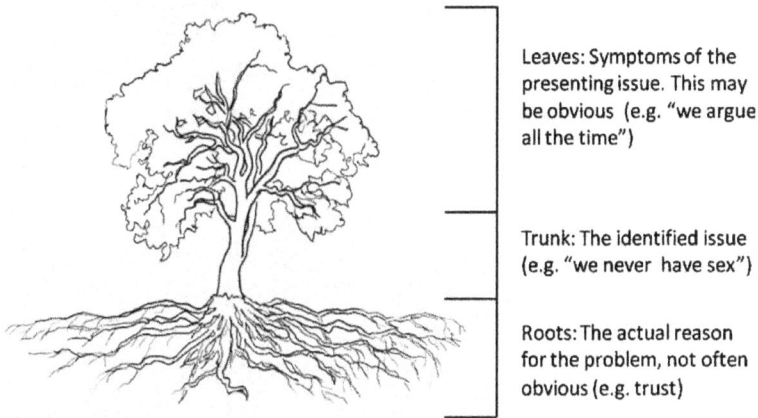

Leaves: Symptoms of the presenting issue. This may be obvious (e.g. "we argue all the time")

Trunk: The identified issue (e.g. "we never have sex")

Roots: The actual reason for the problem, not often obvious (e.g. trust)

DECODE SYMPTOMS WITH 5-WHY ANALYSIS

When you have a problem at work, how do you address it? Do you jump straight in and treat the symptoms, or do you stop and consider whether there's a deeper problem that needs your attention? If you only fix the symptom of an issue — that is, what you see on the surface — and not the root cause of the issue, the problem will almost certainly return and need fixing again.[44] Conversely,

---

44 Rabe, C. B. (2006). *The Innovation killer: How what we know limits what we can imagine—and what smart companies are doing about it.* New York, NY: AMACOM, a Division of the American Management Association.

if you look deeper to determine the source of the problem, you can fix the underlying processes and completely eradicate the issue.

Tactics such as 5-Why Analysis and the Fishbone diagrams often found in Lean Six Sigma approaches to productivity can also be effective tools for deciphering issues in the business world and in your personal life.[45] Toyota developed the 5-Why Analysis method to solve defects in its vehicle process lines. The technique can help you diagnose the root cause of any problem by asking questions that explore the underlying cause-and-effect relationships. For this reason, it's an effective tool to navigate the most significant issues in your marriage.

By repeatedly asking the question "Why?" you can peel back the layers of symptoms that mask the root cause of the problem. Very often, the reason for the problem will lead you to another question, so ask yourself "Why?" five separate times to achieve optimum results.

5-Whys... *the diagram*

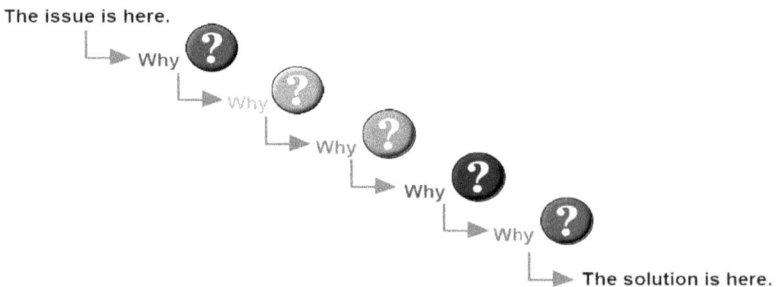

The issue is here.
└─▶ Why ❓
    └─▶ Why ❓
        └─▶ Why ❓
            └─▶ Why ❓
                └─▶ Why ❓
                    └─▶ The solution is here.

---

45 Barry, C. (2011). *Lean marriage tips II: Using 5-why analysis and fishbone diagrams for problem-solving. Retrieved from http://blog.minitab.com/blog/real-world-quality-improvement/lean-marriage-tips-ii.*

BENEFITS OF 5-WHY ANALYSIS

- It helps identify the root cause of the problem.

- It determines the relationship between different root causes of the problem.

- It is a simple tool — easy to use without statistical analysis.

- It is especially useful for problems involving human factors or interactions.

- It can be used in daily life.

When I have someone come to my office to address a presenting issue, I often conduct 5-Why Analysis within the context of the session, such that the client does not recognize the line of questioning.

Using test-taking anxiety in the example below, the 5 Whys might look similar to the following:

Client: I don't know why I am always anxious about the GMAT test. I study and study, feel like I know the material, and then get in the test and freeze. My mind goes blank.

Dr. Lisa: What might happen if you don't do well on the GMAT?

Client: I won't get into graduate school.

Dr. Lisa: Then what?

Client: If I don't get into graduate school, I won't get my MBA.

Dr. Lisa: Then what will happen?

Client: If I don't get my MBA, I won't get a good job. I'll end up bartending or serving for the rest of my life.

Dr. Lisa: Is that the worst-case scenario? What will happen next?

Client: Nobody will want to marry me.

Dr. Lisa: Then what?

Client: I will end up living with my parents.

Dr. Lisa: Then what?

Client: They will get old, and I will move in with them and never have a life of my own. Or worse, I will end up homeless.

In this example, what appeared to be test anxiety was in actuality a fear of what the GMAT represents — having a good job, and therefore, having a life and getting married. When the person enters the test-taking environment, she becomes what I call "emotionally hijacked" with concerns that she will not have a full life if she does not earn her MBA. By taking the client's fear of not having a good life, and decoupling it from the idea that an MBA is the only way she can achieve her goals, then the client's anxiety will decrease. By changing her perspective, she will no longer equate failing the test with not having a full life.

5-Why Analysis is even more emotionally-charged in marital situations. This is because behavior, or lack thereof, has a great deal of meaning.

5-WHY ANALYSIS IN TERMS OF YOUR MARRIAGE

When consulting with couples the evaluation of a presenting issue by breaking it down into composite series of reasons "why" often helps to identify the underlying problem. Couples can also do this on their own, outside of the consultant's office, to get to the root of the issues affecting their marriage. I caution that for couples, it is best to engage in this type of evaluation once heated emotions have passed — at a time when both parties are able to think rationally about their relationship, without feeling inhibited by the circumstances that led to their situation.

Here are the steps couples can take to conduct 5-Why Analysis for their marriage:

1. Write down a specific problem. Writing the issue down will help you formalize the problem and describe it from every angle.

2. Ask yourself why the problem has occurred. Then write the answer below the problem.

3. If the answer you provided doesn't identify the root cause of the problem you wrote down in Step 1, ask why again, and write that answer down.

4. Loop back to Step 3 with your spouse until you identify and agree on the root cause of the problem you are facing.

Generally, asking five "why" questions about your initial problem will quickly reveal the source of the issue. While you may find you need fewer than the suggested five questions to get to the root of the problem, there may also be times when you find yourself asking more than five such questions.

Consider the following example. John and James do not have sufficient financial means and are in need of more money. Each of them conducts 5-Why Analysis to generate a solution.

John: I need more money than I currently have!
Why? Because my job doesn't pay me enough.
Why? Because I can't move up in the company.
Why? Because they want a degree, and I don't have one.
Why? Because I don't have the money to get a degree.
Why? Because of this dead-end job and lack of money, since I cannot move up in the company!

John's problem appears to be his job. Although having a degree would be nice, finding a different job is likely the key to solving his problem. He could find a job that doesn't require a degree to move up within the company, or he could find a job that reimburses employees for their education. Perhaps he could find the same job at a different company, with higher compensation. Or he could parlay his experience into a completely different job, or even another industry. And if John cannot find a better job, he will then know his next option is to further his education.

Meanwhile, James's circumstances reveal a different spin on the "why":

James: We need more money than we currently have!
Why? Because we can't afford to pay our bills.
Why? Because our mortgage is really high.
Why? Because we live in a higher-end neighborhood.
Why? Because we want our kids to attend a good school.
Why? Because they're smart and we want to ensure their future.

James's problem initially sounded like a housing issue, but the reality is that it's rooted in his concerns for providing his children with good educational opportunities. That said, there are certainly choices he could make to change his situation. Could he find a less expensive home in the same area? Could he save enough money in a more modest neighborhood to pay for private school tuition, or perhaps homeschool or private tutors? Could James sublet a room to a college student or take on a second job? Could he ask for a raise and earn more money at his current job? Just like John, James too has options.

5 WHYS WITH SHELBY AND MIKE

"Why" questions reveal how specific circumstances came to be. They allow us to break situations down into causes and effects that we can link together, and ultimately use to create a chain of events that led the couple to seek help in the first place. Shelby and Mike's emotionally-charged marital situation further illustrates the effects of 5-Why Analysis.

When Shelby and Mike stepped inside my office for their first session, our conversation went as follows:

Mike: I had an affair. *(The problem)*

Dr. Lisa: Why did you have an affair? *(Ask why)*

Mike: I don't know. I was at my colleague's house working late on a project and it just happened. *(The answer)*

Dr. Lisa: Why did you go to her house in the first place? She was separated from her husband, so surely you knew there was some risk in being alone with her. Why not go to your place of work or your own home? *(Ask why)*

Mike: I am embarrassed by my home. I didn't want to bring my colleague there because her home is always clean, and it feels good to be there. Not like mine. *(Answer)*

Dr. Lisa: Why do you think your house is a mess? Is this a new development? *(Ask why)*

Mike: I don't know — Shelby stays home all day, and the kids are small, so there is no reason for the house to be a mess. It was never a mess before we had kids, and Shelby always took care of herself back then. She would get dressed every day, keep things tidy. *(Answer)*

Shelby: If you were home more often, you would see that Johnny is a handful. It is really hard to do anything at home when he throws fits all day. I am always tired and can hardly make it through the day, let alone clean, fix dinner, or have sex. *(Answer)*

Dr. Lisa: Why is Johnny a handful? Is this a new development? *(Ask why)*

Shelby: Johnny started having behavioral problems around the time Mike started working longer hours. And now it turns out he was not even at work, but having an affair. I am trying to manage the day-to-day, but I feel like I cannot do anything right. Mike always seems to focus on what I didn't do, even when I accomplish other things. Before I know it, it is the end of the day, and I have not even had a chance to take a shower, much less clean the house. *(Answer)*

Mike: I didn't feel like you wanted me anymore, Shelby. We used to connect. You cared about your appearance and the house. Now you say you are "tired" and don't want anything to do with me. After a while I got tired of hearing "no" whenever I wanted to have sex with you. I grew sick of helping around the house when it did not seem to make any difference. You didn't keep it clean even when I did help. I felt like you didn't care anymore, so why should I? *(Answer)*

By dissecting down to the "why" of how the couple got to the impasse the real reason for the issue can be remedied. For instance. There are a number of "root causes" one can surmise from Shelby and Mike's situation. The presenting issue is an affair. Of course, that in itself is problematic. But rather than focusing on the affair, Shelby and Mike explored the events and feelings leading up to the betrayal. By shedding light on the "roots" that needed to be addressed, Mike realized the situation culminating in the affair was in part the convenience of being at his colleague's home. But at some point in his thought process, he also felt the idea of "why care?" gave him license to act.

Underlying the situation was Mike's perception that Shelby "didn't care" anymore. As you saw in the above conversation, this was inaccurate — she was in survival mode and felt like a single parent since Mike was often gone. On some level, she was also angry and hurt that Mike was spending so much time away, which made her feel less connected to him. This did not do much for their intimate life.

What happened next?

Once they both agreed they wanted their marriage to work, Shelby and Mike delved into the process of change. Johnny was referred to another clinician who agreed their concerns were valid, and both parents joined forces and learned new skills that helped them better manage their son's behavior. They then enrolled Johnny in a special school that worked with his academic strengths and helped him regulate his emotions.

In addition, Shelby and Mike hired someone to clean the house each week. They continued our consultation relationship and focused on challenging their perceptions of the circumstances leading up to their marital troubles. Moreover, rather than acting on partial information or assumptions, they began expressing what they felt. They stopped blaming each other for their struggles, and began taking action to address the root cause of every issue. This was largely accomplished by pausing before speaking and listening to the other person's perspective before responding, which allowed both parties to feel heard and validated.

In order to identify the source of a problem, you need to dig deep and ask yourself "Why?" Only then, once you have broken the problem down into its composite parts, can you begin the real work of changing your behavior.

By seeing the composite parts, you and your spouse can then discover how you are each putting particular pieces of the puzzle into action. You must contribute to the problem, take responsibility for your respective parts, and position yourselves to act differently in the future to achieve different results. Overall, you can decide to work toward a successful marriage, or choose to act in such a way that you maintain the same dissatisfying relationship.

Remember that the choices you make are a direct reflection of your values — of what you consider most important in your life. If you value your relationship, then after breaking down the problem you can identify which underlying issues are a product of your choices, and you can begin to act differently. Joe and Leslie are another pertinent example of value based choices in action.

CASE STUDY — JOE AND LESLIE

Leslie arrived at my office and indicated that Joe was "supposed to be arriving any minute." Joe did not show, so Leslie and I talked through some of the concerns she believed Joe had with her.

Most recently, Leslie had come home to find Joe had moved all of his personal belongings out of the house, and even taken the family dog. Leslie had called Joe on numerous occasions to discuss his unexpected departure, but her husband would not tell her where he had taken residence. Instead, he said, "You know what you did."

By the third session, it was evident that Joe did not want to reconcile. Even though he had originally told Leslie to "work on herself," and then they could "get back together," talk of this nature had ceased. Joe was furious with Leslie for telling her parents he had moved out, citing that she was "making him out to be the bad guy" even though he had left because of "what she had done." It came to light that Leslie had taken out credit cards, maxing them out to purchase new clothes and suits after receiving a sizeable promotion in state government, as she was due to be a running mate in the next gubernatorial election.

Joe had previously served as a high-ranking military officer, but was forced to retire after sustaining complicated physical injuries in deployment. While he was on active duty, Leslie was a homemaker, and they had both agreed this was best for their children since they moved frequently as a result of his military career. Leslie managed to extract enough information from Joe to deduce that his anger toward her had really begun when she spent money to go back to school approximately five years before.

Leslie had enjoyed a very quick trajectory in politics and state government, and while Joe never stated it explicitly, it appeared he resented his wife for the success she enjoyed. He dismissed her when she wanted to discuss her day, and would disregard anything of merit she shared regarding her career.

In theory, maxing out their credit cards without telling Joe was a poor choice Leslie made, but Leslie explained that she couldn't talk to her husband about clothes or her work without starting a severe argument. Looking deeper, it became clear the purchases were merely a symptom of a greater issue — Joe's lack of support.

Looking at Leslie and Joe, the values that led to their marital discord were not immediately evident. Was it that Joe didn't want Leslie to have a career, or was it that he felt like she valued it over her relationship with him? Perhaps Joe missed his own career, and Leslie's success made him feel ashamed.

In turn, did Leslie value a new wardrobe and work opportunities over honesty in her marriage, or did she simply want peace and hoped to avoid an argument? The answers to these questions are complicated. As stated previously they are not to be found in absolutes or "black and white" thinking. The case of Dawn and Alan further illustrates this point, along with the concept of values and behavior alignment.

CASE STUDY — DAWN AND ALAN

Dawn felt her husband Alan had been growing increasingly distant. It was as if she and their daughter didn't have a place in his life. In their first session, he stated he wanted to work on their marriage, that he didn't want it to be over, and that he wanted their life to be different.

What I found to be remarkable was that every point made through the marital sessions, Alan acknowledged the issue being that he was distant, often not fully mentally present, that his mindshare had been on his job, that he did not communicate, and that he made decisions without Dawn's input. He indicated that at times, he did not want to argue, so he would passively acquiesce but be angry and take out how he felt in other ways. Two of these ways were through how he spent his time (i.e., away from Dawn) and how he spent his money (i.e., not on her).

Alan was in his mid-forties. About four years prior, his physician had told him he needed to get healthy or he was going to die of a heart attack, stroke, etc. So Alan started spending considerable time in the gym and making friends with younger guys, many of whom were either unmarried or recently divorced. Additionally, Alan resurrected his passion for music. He started playing guitar and joined a band.

Dawn kept the budget, and Alan admitted he was not good with money and that Dawn was better at keeping the finances together. So Alan would have to come to Dawn to talk about major purchases. She had become the gatekeeper of the family money, which made Alan feel resentful. But Alan would not talk with Dawn about this resentment.

Dawn would show Alan the figures and clearly detail where they were already spending their money. Then she and Alan would agree on how discretionary funds needed to be spent. Later Alan would come home and either ask Dawn if there were financial resources to do something or just go out and make the purchase, and then Dawn would have to clean up whatever financial mess he made as a result of his purchase.

To Dawn's face Alan was fine with the way their resources were being allocated. However, behaviorally he revealed he was not okay. He seemed to have decided he was going to do what he wanted to do, regardless of whether the resources were available. Alan's retort was that they had always been able to figure it out, even with his purchases, so he began to think that Dawn's control was really misplaced and that their circumstances were not as dire as she had portrayed.

Alan continued purchasing new amps, new guitars. He spent increasing amounts of time away from home at band practice, some of which were held forty-five minutes away from their residence, sometimes four to five times per week.

Keep in mind they had a teenage daughter, and Dawn had lupus, so she was not as active or able to work as much as she had prior to her illness. The financial resources were diminishing, but Alan's activities were not decreasing — weekends with the band, trying to play gigs, "taking the band to the next level," and frequent stops at the bar.

Alan continued to take time away from the family. Dawn had expressed early on that the genre of music Alan played was not her taste. This had set up a situation where when Dawn would ask to be a part of his life, Alan would respond, "You don't like my kind of music, so why should I ask you if you want to come to the bar or watch us practice?"

Dawn would counter, "I want to be at least asked, so I can have the choice."

Alan would then retort, "Why should I waste my time asking when I know it will just be 'no,' or you will get angry for my going to practice at all?"

During appointments, Alan would commit to do better and include Dawn in his decisions regarding when he would go to practice and what he would purchase — but outside of our sessions, his behavior was not any different.

The presenting issue was Dawn's complaint that Alan did not spend enough time with the family. Looking deeper, Dawn believed "the band" was more important to Alan than she and their daughter. Alan also felt Dawn's disapproval of him, of what he was doing with the band, and ultimately of his dreams of having a successful band, albeit later in life. Instead of engaging her to participate or come to his practices, Alan simply wanted to "avoid an argument" by doing whatever he wanted, which would turn into an argument when he eventually returned home, often at two or three in the morning. Alan also resented Dawn because he felt like she was a "mother" to him and he did not feel it was necessary that he "check in" with her.

Although Alan would say he wanted things to be different, his behavior was clearly contradictory. He chose to spend his free time with the band, younger comrades, and others, rather than with his wife and daughter. He chose to spend money on purchases he wanted to make without considering the household needs. Behaviorally we see that he valued the band and his activities more than he did his wife and child, despite his assertions to the contrary.

THE TWO-WAY STREET

Viewing your spouse as the source of your marital problems is a common antecedent to divorce, and doesn't take into account the roles both partners play in the relationship. The habits spouses develop over the years go with them when they walk out the door. This may in part account for the saddening statistic that 60 percent of second marriages also end in divorce.[46] Without actively changing our behavior, we have a tendency to fall back on old habits.

GETTING AT THE HEART OF THE PROBLEM

Of note — I don't follow the idea that couples can overcome their marital problems by gaining insights into their childhood traumas. Psychoanalytic theory implies that this is the case, and that once the root of the problem is identified and worked through, the problem will disappear. While this approach works for certain couples, experience has taught me that these insights take too long for relationships in crisis. Couples on the brink of divorce require immediate evidence of the "light at the end of the tunnel" to escape the all-consuming pessimism known to dissolve relationships.

Another detour on the road to problem-solving? Early in my career I had a belief that couples must understand how their upbringing influences behaviors and attitudes in marriage. While this perspective was often interesting and sometimes informative, my clients would frequently plead, "Now I see that we are reenacting our

---

46 Gottman, J. M. (2014). *What predicts divorce?: The relationship between marital processes and marital outcomes.* Hove, UK: Psychology Press.

parents' marriages, but what do we do about it? We can't stop fighting." I learned that explaining others' problems doesn't necessarily solve them, and that solutions are far more important. This pursuit of solutions was a catalyst for the EMS.

By now the reader can see that one needs to look underneath the expressed problems — the symptoms — and examine the underlying problems. This is done by becoming aware of process over subject matter, of the *how* over the *what*. When we look at process in conversations, we can almost always improve our communication. Pay close attention to these four steps:

1. Try to understand your partner's point of view.
Focus on what your spouse is telling you. Rather than convincing them to change their mind, put yourself in their shoes and listen to what they are saying.

2. Reflect on your own feelings.
Throughout the conversation, examine how you and your partner are making each other feel. Do you feel threatened by what they are saying? Does your spouse say they feel uneasy about what you are telling them? Rather than correcting your spouse or getting defensive, take a deep breath. Fight the urge to cut your partner off, and reflect on your emotions. This will enhance your communication.

3. Focus on understanding instead of being understood.[47]
Do what you can to empathize with your spouse. Our feelings are more reflexive than they are logical, emotionally rooted rather than linear. Keep in mind that while your partner's feelings may not

47 Covey, S. (1989). *The seven habits of highly successful people. New York, NY: Fireside/Simon & Schuster.*

make sense to you, your partner is genuinely experiencing them, and that's worth acknowledging.

4. Make sure your spouse knows you want to understand their perspective.

In your own words, state what you believe your spouse is saying. Ask questions as needed, and let them know you want to understand their thoughts and feelings. When tensions are high, a little acknowledgement can help diffuse a stressful situation. Avoid being combative, even if you disagree with what your spouse is saying. You might say, "You think I should spend less time on the golf course?" or "It sounds like you feel very discouraged. How can I help?" Listen to your partner, and show them you care about addressing the challenges in your relationship.

In all four of the steps, it is not what you or your spouse is saying that is most important. Rather, it is your joint ability to pay attention to *how* you communicate that matters here — *how* you speak and listen to each another, *how* you each feel during the conversation, and *how* you respond. By creating a process for interacting in a way that promotes respect, love, and listening, particularly when you and your spouse are voicing your frustrations, you can build trust and tackle the underlying issues in your marriage.

KEY TAKEAWAYS

- Both spouses play a role in the marriage. Avoid placing blame on the other person, and acknowledge how you and your partner can work together more productively.

- "Waiting out" a rough patch is hardly effective. For things to get better, you must join forces with your spouse and come up with a concrete action plan. Rather than blaming the other person, focus on moving forward.

- Explore the underlying problems in your relationship. Look past what you see on the surface, and assess the root causes of the issues you are facing to achieve a long-term fix.

NEXT UP

A clear theme in this book is the importance of differentiating between the presenting symptoms and the true, underlying cause of the conflict in your marriage. By slowing down and establishing a deliberate process for communicating, you and your spouse will gain more opportunities to get at the heart of the issues you are facing.

To explore this in more detail, in the following chapters we will look at additional case studies in which the presenting symptom — the glaring *what* that brought the couple to seek help in the first place — had to be carefully parsed in order to uncover the source of the conflict. Once uncovered, the partners still needed to consider whether they each valued the marriage enough to change their behaviors, and ultimately stop the root cause of their problems from repeating the same cycle of pain and frustration.

PART 3

THE DESTINATION
SPARKING CONSCIOUS TRANSFORMATION

7 MAP YOUR MARITAL PERCEPTIONS

To map out a course of action and follow it to an end requires some of the same courage that a soldier needs.

—Ralph Waldo Emerson

As detailed throughout this book, one can see in most cases that the presenting situation is not the main source of marital conflict. While it is almost always more apparent than the underlying cause of the conflict, the actual source of the problem needs to be addressed in order to strengthen the marriage. All relationships have a beginning, middle, and end, with frequent ups and downs. As such, issues of perception often result in spousal discord.

A number of experts consider fighting about money, sex, or children deadly to relationships.[48] I, on the other hand, see these issues as the external manifestation of more fundamental problems in the marriage.

In short, I believe our perception does not necessarily reflect reality. It's not what we intend to say, but how we are perceived that really counts. The *how* supersedes the *what*. In a conflict, the less-skilled parts of both participants tend to take on a protective stance. This often backfires, and the relationship becomes further strained. However, if we can modify the way we see the situation, then we can open ourselves up to change.

CASE STUDY — JUDY AND JIM

Judy and Jim are just one example of the importance of perception in a marriage. The spouses had been married for 10 years, and came into my office with very different perspectives on housework. They experienced a great deal of marital conflict in terms of how they perceived housework, including how it should be done and which components were most important.

Jim believed Judy prioritized her volunteering over the housework, as he would come home to find dishes in the sink on days she volunteered at their son's school. Meanwhile, Judy was angry because Jim often told her how to be organized enough to get both jobs done. In this case, Judy did not hear *what* Jim was

---

48 Gottman, J., & Silver, N. (2015). *The seven principles for making marriage work: A practical guide from the country's foremost relationship expert.* Easton, PA: Harmony.

saying because she did not appreciate *how* he was saying it. She perceived Jim as an enemy rather than a help, and believed her husband was attacking her. Her perception of their interactions mattered most in this exchange.

How can you be sure that your partner is perceiving your intentions correctly? One way is to simply ask, "When I was saying X to you, what were you thinking? How did it make you feel?" It is only in moving past the *what* and exploring *how* each partner in the relationship perceives the other that spouses can tackle their problems and come up with an appropriate solution.

THE MANY MAPS OF A SINGLE TERRITORY

The phrase "the map is not the territory"[49] further illustrates the differences between our beliefs and reality. Connection with one's partner can only be achieved by sympathizing with their point of view on issues that are present in the marriage. Understanding this metaphor is crucial to resolving conflict in an effective manner.

This is because we humans make abstractions all the time. An "abstraction," in this case, is when a person simplifies, condenses, or symbolizes what is going on in order to understand it more clearly. This, they believe, will help them discuss the issue, or even think about it in a better way.

For example, those who drive down the street observe their surroundings at the general level. However, if I am driving and get involved in an accident, my perceptions of the incident will constitute an abstraction. Other people involved in the accident will

---

49 Korzybski, A. (1993). *Science and sanity: An introduction to non-Aristotelian systems and general semantics (5th ed.)*. Englewood, NJ: International Non-Aristotelian Library.

experience the event differently, depending on their vantage point and other sensory data, and no individual will experience more than a portion of what went on. This is because our observations pass through certain filters of perception.

If a bystander witnesses the accident from the sidewalk, they too will form an abstraction about what occurred leading to and immediately after the incident. Likewise, the other motorists involved in the accident will abstract reality differently.

The bystander might recollect, "I saw two cars, a red pickup driving east and a blue Hyundai going west, and the blue car was going to turn left before the red pickup swerved out of its way and deliberately hit it." And while this description might give others an idea of what occurred, the reality of the accident is a very imprecise approximation of what actually took place. Even if the accident appeared to be deliberate, the bystander would have minimal evidence to confirm this information. As such, their perceptions are merely an approximation of what took place. The next day, they might create an even deeper abstraction, and simply say they "witnessed an accident."

If another person recorded this individual's description of the accident, and considered it a factual account of what happened, then a number of misconceptions might arise. It is important to recognize that our observations are only one map, and that different maps can be drawn for the same territory. With this mindset, it will be much easier to reconcile the differences between perception and reality.

The point in this scenario is to illustrate that everyone has their own unique take on reality. When there are two or more perceptions of reality, the facts of the matter are likely a combination of all the different perceptions at play.

In marriage, the same thing applies. The above scenario illustrates that most disagreements stem from a failure to recognize all the factors at play in a given event, as no single map reflects what is truly going on in its entirety.

People argue their points based on their own perception maps. They fail to realize that others use different perception maps, and act as though theirs is the only one in existence. Needless to say, this is a recipe for disaster in a marriage. Couples must make the effort to understand each other's perceptions and points of view.

If someone relocated from New York to California, but continued to use their New York roadmap, would they get acquainted with their new geographic region? Although they might be more familiar with the New York map, and like it better than the California roadmap, the decision to use the incorrect map would almost definitely result in confusion, frustration, and a major lack of efficiency.

With mental maps, we don't always realize we're using a map at all. Our mental maps are not quite as obvious as printed roadmaps because we use them to think our thoughts and feel our feelings — and this typically comes so naturally that we fail to recognize the processes at play. We often confuse our thoughts with the territory. Each of us thinks that the way we see the world *is* the world in its true form, when in fact it is just the way we have mapped it out individually. Our perspective is just an approximation, or an abstraction of reality that we genuinely believe to be true.

By recognizing that "[our] map is not the territory," we can accept our thoughts and feelings for what they are. We can take them with a grain of salt, evaluate them, and change them if other thoughts or feelings arise that would be more objective or healthy. We can improve our maps. And by doing so, we can improve the quality of our lives, our experiences, and our relationships. In a business setting, this same practice can also help us become more successful.

Another situation, illustrative of inaccurate perceptions, reveals how the presenting situation is not the true cause of marital conflict. Note how Tam and Steve have confused their individual maps with the territory of their marriage.

CASE STUDY — TAM AND STEVE

Steve, a high-ranking military officer, accompanied Tam, his wife of nineteen years, to a couples consult. Tam was very quiet on their first visit — she appeared withdrawn, and did not volunteer much information about Steve.

The seemingly obvious problem was that Steve wanted more sex, and that Tam was not giving it to him. Steve claimed that this was the reason for their frequent arguments and overall marital discord.

But the issue was far more complex. The couple had endured years of Steve being deployed and chasing his next special ops mission — a necessary track for a high-ranking military officer. As a result, Tam was left at home to take care of everything else.

Now that Steve had retired from the military, he was home all the time. This highlighted the disconnection between spouses, and prompted the consultation appointment. When I asked Tam and Steve whether counseling was a "last-ditch effort" to save their marriage, Tam indicated that it was. Steve, however, was shocked to hear this, as he had thought the issue was nothing more than a minor disagreement over their sex life.

He explained that when he came home from work or time in the field, he naturally wanted to connect with Tam. And yet, he received a cool reception when he tried to be intimate with her. He could not understand why, since he was a good provider and allowed Tam to stay home rather than work. As such, Steve did not feel appreciated or loved.

This, of course, was merely Steve's perception. Tam had a different take on the matter. From her point of view, Tam felt like she was just an object for Steve to "get off on" when he was home. She claimed he was clueless about how she felt, and even about who she was as a person.

Below the surface, Tam was grappling with years of anger from feeling like a single parent. She felt unappreciated and now resentful that Steve was home and simply expected everything to be great. Tam could also sense his resentment that their children — now teens — would not go to him for parenting matters. She felt that Steve jockeyed for her attention and grew mopey when she prioritized the children's needs.

As a result, Tam did not want to spend time with Steve. To her, it seemed as though Steve was just another child who needed her attention. She was hesitant to show any affection to him because each time she hugged or kissed him, Steve immediately wanted to hit the sheets. Sex felt like another item on her laundry list of chores, and Tam didn't know whether to give in and have sex with her husband, or endure his complaints when she declined.

Of course, the main issue in Tam and Steve's relationship was not their sex life. Their perceptions — the conflicting maps of their marital territory, if you will — were exacerbating the problem.

Steve's perception of the situation: "I am retired now — and I just want to spend time with Tam and let her know I love her. The way I do that is through sex. But she always shuts me down, or isn't really into it."

Tam's perception of the situation: "Steve is just like my kids — he always wants something from me. He is clueless about everything I have to do each day, and now that he's home he does not help much around the house. On the rare occasion he does help, it is his way and not the way I did things for years when he was away from home. We got along fine when he was working, but now that he is retired, he pouts whenever I don't feel like having sex. It's exhausting."

At the end of their initial visit, I asked Tam whether she could commit to being "all in" with Steve. Tam's response was that she could not. She was starting to think she wanted out of the marriage — but she wasn't sure.

My parting thought to her on this initial meeting was, "You cannot simultaneously prepare for divorce and work on your marriage." It was not my job to convince her to stay or go, but one thing was clear. Before she and Steve could do meaningful work on their relationship, she had to make a decision. Tam's homework assignment was to decide whether she would commit to repairing her marriage.

Similarly, Steve's homework was to cease being another child — to actually see what he could do to help with the children and the household, and be an active marital participant rather than another drain on the system.

About a month later, the couple returned for another session. Tam seemed less guarded and expressed that she had been able to kiss and hug Steve without feeling like he would take these forms of affection as license to "run to the bedroom." In addition, Steve had been helping more around the house — but he had gone from one end of the spectrum to the other. Now Steve was doing everything, and not necessarily the way Tam wanted. For years, Tam had managed the house and the kids, and she believed her system was better than her husband's.

Tam expressed that she felt Steve was not thinking about *what* she needed, but what he *thought* she needed. In Steve's attempt to improve his understanding of their marital problems, and acknowledge that there was more at play than a sex issue, he assumed that Tam wanted him to do all the housework. And while Steve knew that his map of the territory was different from Tam's, he still didn't create the bridge and make the connection that Tam needed.

In short, the couple needed to focus on the *how* over the *what*. For example, Steve could inquire, "Tam, how can I support you with the housework?" He could ask his wife, "When I do all the dishes and help cook dinner, am I helping you? Or is there a better way I can contribute?"

Nonetheless, Tam disclosed that she was committed to the marriage. While she was not convinced that Steve had truly changed, and she didn't know whether her husband was simply going through the motions of helping out in order to appease her, things were improving.

Superficially, one might suggest that Tam and Steve work on their marriage by scheduling more frequent date nights, or by pursuing another approach that would promote intimacy in their marriage. That said, rather than rushing to implement a solution to the presenting problem, it is important for each spouse to clarify the other's perception of reality.

Tam and Steve held their own perceptions of reality, and needed to acknowledge their differences in order to bridge the gap in their communication. Focusing on their process — the *how* instead of the *what* — helped them improve their connection.

PERCEPTION AND CONTROL

Of course, perception is a complex notion. In the workplace, many executives have a keen perception of control, and closely monitor the strategies within the company that drive profits and minimize costs.

This same mindset of control is common in marriage, and it is an issue I often see in my practice. Control of money, financial arrangements, and sex — even the direction the toilet paper is put on the roll — are all presenting concerns that have entered my office.

In particular, there are two scenarios of control in a marital setting: one, the spouse that is perceived as being controlling is actually oblivious to how their partner views them and their approach to situations, and two, the "controlling" person has legitimate control issues rooted in their family of origin.

Family of origin issues are beyond the scope of this book. That said, the following case study illustrates how one spouse might be oblivious to how they are exerting control over their partner.

CASE STUDY — DIRK AND GLORIA

Dirk and Gloria were in a fifteen-year committed relationship, with three children under the age of ten. Gloria worked as a successful attorney at a large law firm, while Dirk was a stay-at-home dad. Dirk was employed when he met Gloria, but injured his back several years into their relationship.

Once he got off disability, Dirk opted not to return to work. The couple decided to start their family around this time, with Dirk serving as the primary caretaker for the children.

After the birth of their first child, Dirk developed a close relationship with one of the mothers in the neighborhood. They spent a lot of time together, drinking coffee and talking while their children played together. When Gloria questioned Dirk about the friendship, he became angry and accused his wife of being possessive and unreasonable. Gloria dropped the issue until she found a receipt for an expensive bracelet Dirk had given his supposed "friend." Dirk continued to deny any kind of relationship with the neighbor, Gloria let it go, and over time Dirk's friendship with the neighbor cooled.

From the beginning of their relationship, Gloria's friends and family told her how controlling Dirk was. He monitored everything Gloria did, and complained when she had to work overtime or go on a business trip. This controlling behavior was obvious to their friends, as Dirk would say these things in front of them. If they went out for dinner, for example, and Gloria ordered dessert, Dirk would tell her she didn't need it. In turn, if Gloria wanted to buy a new pair of shoes or a suit for work, Dirk would tell her she was a spendthrift and their budget wouldn't allow for it.

It was obvious to everyone who knew the couple that Dirk was in control on every front. Even in parenting, he was strict with the children and contradicted Gloria in front of the kids when she tried to be more lenient.

Three years after the birth of their last child, Dirk became close friends with a woman he met at the kids' soccer games. They began to spend more time together, as their children played on the same team. Dirk and the other woman went out to lunch after soccer, and sometimes took their children to the movies if Gloria was out of town or working late. Gloria confronted Dirk on his attachment to this new female friend, and again, Dirk became outraged and accused Gloria of being a hypocrite because she didn't think men and women could be just friends. He seemed oblivious to the control he was exerting over his wife.

Dirk went on to discuss Gloria's friendships with the male attorneys at her firm, reminding her that she had lunch with them and even traveled with them on occasion. Gloria backed off because she believed Dirk had a point, and maybe she did have a double standard. However, when she noticed credit card charges for women's apparel and jewelry she knew she didn't purchase, she confronted Dirk. He was rather matter of fact about buying the other woman new clothes because her husband was struggling financially; he stated that he was just helping out a friend.

Gloria again backed off, but when she discussed the situation with her friends, they were adamant that she was being taken advantage of. They thought Dirk was lying and spending too much time and money on the other woman. Besides, they said, her relationship wasn't healthy.

There are control issues evident in this case. Some executive women similar to Gloria are extremely capable in their career, but insecure on a personal level. In short, many women like Gloria have difficulty asserting themselves in the marital union. In this case, Dirk took advantage of Gloria's inability to be more self-assertive. Additionally, Dirk bestowed what modicum of support and positive energy he had on women other than his wife. The relationships he fostered with other women were fulfilling needs that should have stayed within the marriage.

At the other end of a spectrum, the presence of a controlling partner may also prompt the *non-controlling* spouse to seek intimacy elsewhere. This is what happened to Suzy and Bobby.

CASE STUDY — SUZY AND BOBBY

Bobby was the successful CEO of an investment banking institution. Suzy, his wife, did not work outside the home. On the surface, the couple appeared to have everything — two healthy children, plenty of money, a sprawling estate in the country, and several horses. They were also active in their church and local philanthropic organizations.

What brought them to my office was Bobby's evidence that "he knew" Suzy was having an affair. Exploring the issue further, Bobby had deduced that Suzy was being unfaithful because she was spending considerable time at the barn with their daughter while the daughter took riding lessons. "You are always at the barn," Bobby would say, visibly angry at Suzy for dismissing his accusations.

Bobby thought Suzy was spending time "with everyone else" but him, and that she was acting differently toward him. Bobby had come home from work three days prior, and Suzy had announced she was leaving because "she [didn't] love him" anymore.

Delving deeper into the presenting issue in their marriage, there was a plethora of underlying concerns affecting their relationship. Suzy did not like Bobby; she found him controlling and believed that he did not value her contributions as a wife.

Control was an issue from early in their marriage. When the couple endured financial losses during the 2008 market crash, Bobby filed for bankruptcy to avoid losing the family home. Rather than telling Suzy, he became very controlling about their financial situation, scrutinizing every purchase and questioning the need for every item — even groceries — that Suzy brought home. Bobby also spent most of his time at the office trying to salvage his business.

The more Bobby exerted his control over their finances, the more resentful Suzy became. She not only continued to spend their money, but Suzy also grew more reckless with her purchases. "If he was going to treat me like a child, I was going to do as I pleased," she explained.

Suzy also felt justified in spending their money because Bobby was never home.

Suzy became immersed in her daughter's equestrian career, and Bobby continued questioning her about the money she spent. As time went on, Suzy continued pulling away from Bobby because she believed all he wanted to do was control her. She also felt that Bobby did not see her and the kids as a priority because he spent all his time at the office, and when he was home, he worked on his computer and was not mentally present with the family.

In fact, Bobby was so consumed by his business, and so desperate to maintain his affluent lifestyle, that he had failed to notice his wife retreating from their marriage. Suzy started talking with other mothers at the barn, and one of the coaches her daughter was working with took notice of her. Suzy said that she had begun to feel "like herself again" around this trainer. She felt comfortable in his presence — he was not at all controlling — and Suzy wanted to spend as much time as she could at the barn.

Suzy wanted to help her daughter hone her equestrian skills, but also spend time with the man for whom she now had feelings.

Eventually Bobby hired a private investigator who caught Suzy with the trainer. Until he presented hard evidence to her, Suzy continued to deny the extramarital affair. Once she admitted to the betrayal, Bobby was angry and hurt — he ran the gauntlet of emotions while Suzy appeared very cool and almost smug. She implied that Bobby deserved it, and that she had done no wrong.

When this all came to light during their session, I asked the bottom-line question: "Do you want to work out your relationship, or is it over?" I told the couple that they had to get clear on their answer to this question both individually and collectively, and explained that while I did not espouse divorce as the best option, it was not my job to convince them to work through the issues that were present long before the affair occurred.

If Bobby and Suzy wanted their marriage to work, they needed to sort through the underlying issues we identified during our consultation. Bobby moved out of the master bedroom while he was deciding on the fate of his marriage. Suzy, meanwhile, had ended the affair and only saw the trainer in passing at the barn.

Again, the affair might seem like the obvious problem in Bobby and Suzy's relationship, but it was only a symptom of many more substantial issues. Affairs are akin to an opportunistic infection in a terminally-ill patient. The infection is a dangerous side problem that must be eradicated swiftly and completely — but it is not the root problem. Take away the infection, and the disease remains.

Similarly, unmet needs might account for why a marriage was unhappy or susceptible to an affair, but they never explain the affair itself. Even if the affair ends, if you do not address the emotional problems at play in your marriage, you will still have a broken relationship. The affair is not the root problem.

And while Bobby desperately wanted to save his marriage, he was fixated on Suzy's affair. He could not fathom that there were other factors affecting his relationship. His perception of control did not align with his wife's, who felt judged by her husband and found solace in the arms of a more welcoming man.

Bobby had approached EMS consultation with great pride, wanting to be "right" at all costs and exonerated from any role in where the marriage was headed. For this marital situation to change, Bobby had to consider the conditions that predisposed Suzy to the affair, and thus, take a certain degree of responsibility. He had to decide between being right and staying married. Suzy too had to be "all in" and make an effort to reconcile.

To speak in terms of "the map is not the territory," the affair constituted Bobby's map of his marital territory with Suzy. However, it was only a small piece of Suzy's map. In order for the spouses to reconnect, they needed to recognize each other's individual maps and create a bridge between them. Here again we return to the crucial role of personal responsibility, and the importance of addressing the root cause of the problem in order to rectify a marriage.

KEY TAKEAWAYS

- The presenting situation is rarely the main source of marital conflict. While it is usually more visible than the underlying cause, the source needs to be addressed in order to make improvements.

- This is why it is so important to explore issues of perception. These issues often lead to spousal discord, as both partners have their own unique take on reality. The truth is usually somewhere between both spouses' perceptions.

- Affairs are not all that different than an opportunistic infection in someone who is already terminally ill. While the infection must be cured, it is not the root problem — even without the infection, the disease remains.

NEXT UP

By now the act of examining how your actions, values, and beliefs contribute to your marriage should be apparent. However, this practice is quite foreign to CEOs. Why? Because the CEO sits in a command position where they can demand that others modify their actions and behaviors to align with their approach.

But just because this works at the office, doesn't mean that it's effective at home. For the marriage to flourish, the CEO must step down from this commanding stance in their personal relationships.

8 CHOOSE TO CHANGE

By changing nothing, nothing changes.

—Tony Robbins

In my experience helping executives work on their marriages, I've found that many CEOs believe others should change just because they tell them to. While this approach may bring success within business, it does not work in marriage. For an intimate relationship to succeed, the executive must go back to basics, get real, take a hard look at their own actions, and make a conscious decision to change. Choosing to change means that executives must park their pride and recognize that they have a role in the current state of their marriage. Consequently, if they want their marriage to succeed, they too must learn to think and act differently.

FINDING COMMON GROUND

Many couples who come to me indicate that they "cannot communicate." Communication, however, is as abstract a concept as someone stating they "just want to be happy." In its most basic definition, communication is a "two-way process of reaching mutual understanding in which participants not only exchange information, news, ideas, and feelings but also create and share meaning."[50]

To communicate, a person must "construct a mental picture of something (e.g., a 'concept'), give it a name, and develop a feeling about it."[51] Effective communication with another person implies that the concept, the name, and the feeling reflect the other person's interpretations. In other words, effective communication requires a shared understanding of where the other person is coming from, and that we refer to the same things when we speak.

Of course, most people believe they communicate well. Management and communication consultants say that more than 10 percent of U.S. business enterprises fail each year "primarily because

---

50 Goldhaber, G. M. (1993). *Organizational communication.* Madison, WI: Brown & Benchmark.

51 *Ibid.*

of bad management and ineffective employee communication."[52] Therefore, communication is not only a major challenge for many otherwise-successful executives, but it is also a source of disconnect.

In order to change how we communicate, we must change our approach. Both at home and at work, we must think differently and listen more than we speak. There is a purpose to having two ears and one mouth — this distribution allows us to listen twice as much as we speak.

And yet, for some people talking *is* good communication — but only if they are speaking. For these individuals, good communication is all about conveying what they want to say in a clear, effective manner. But communication involves so much more than actively emitting sound waves. It is most powerful from a non-judgmental point of view, with the intent of understanding the other parties involved in the discussion.

The most powerful aspects of communication are listening to understand and speaking to clarify.

Powerful communication is accomplished without pride — without the ego getting in the way. Pride often drives the addition of a critical commentary in the form of negative cognitions, also known as "thinking errors," which are rarely beneficial.

This means that judgment often takes place during someone else's narrative, and this prideful, arrogant approach distorts or silences the other person's intent.

If you have a reply sitting ready in your mind, or if you sense a reply taking shape when someone else is speaking, then you are

---

52 *Ibid.*

not truly listening. And as a result, you are not communicating as well as you could be. The brain is a single-channel device; it is either receiving or sending information. Two thoughts cannot reside in the mind simultaneously while listening. In other words, you cannot think of a retort to what your spouse is saying and still actively listen to their point of view.

The first and most difficult part of marital communication involves leaving your pride at the door and listening with an open spirit. Being receptive to what your partner is saying promotes inquiry, which can then lead to mutual understanding:

- What is it you see that I don't?

- How do you see this differently and why?

- Please help me understand your perspective.

In order to ask these questions, you cannot focus on having the "best" or "last" answer. Overcoming the impulse to have the last word is crucial to improving your communication. In turn, expanding your understanding is more important than being right or getting your point across.

FIGHTING FAIRLY

There are countless books and therapeutic approaches to "fighting fairly," and the bottom line is this: successful long-term relationships have their fair share of conflict. Conflict is a natural component of emotional intimacy.

But too many people shy away from raising their voices or asserting their needs. There are multiple reasons for this, including fear of abandonment, a belief that fighting is a sign of weakness, or simply a desire to not be like other couples who are constantly screaming at each other.

At the other extreme are couples who cannot control their emotions — couples for whom every day brings a new, explosive battle. And of course, there are also relationships where one partner is a fighter and the other a peacekeeper.

And in terms of your natural disposition, there is no right or wrong answer. Anger is part of the human condition, and can push us to break free from negative situations. Every healthy relationship involves conflict. One leading relationship psychologist believes that "Fighting . . . can be one of the healthiest things a couple can do for their relationship." In his book, he says how you fight is "one of the most telling ways to diagnose the health of your marriage."[53]

That said, when anger occurs over a long period of time, resentment and bitterness result.

THE NATURE OF A "HEALTHY" MARRIAGE[54]

One relationship expert[55] indicates that to sustain a stable marriage, there must be five times as many positive moments together as there are negative ones. Most couples, he believes, simply want love and respect. And while this may sound simple, in *Seven Prin-*

---

53 Gottman, J., Gottman, J. M., & Silver, N. (1995). *Why marriages succeed or fail: And how you can make yours last. Simon and Schuster.*

54 Gottman, J. M., Gottman, J., & Silver, N. (2015). *The seven principles for making marriage work: A practical guide from the country's foremost relationship expert. Harmony.*

55 Burgoyne, C. B., Reibstein, J., Edmunds, A. M., & Routh, D. A. (2010). *Marital commitment, money and marriage preparation: What changes after the wedding?. Journal of Community & Applied Social Psychology, 20(5), 390-403.*

ciples of a Healthy Marriage,[56] John Gottman points out that if she doesn't feel loved, a woman will not act respectfully toward her husband. In turn, by not feeling respected, the man will act without love.

Consider a couple twenty-eight years into their marriage. Respect, trust, and honor have consistently been the pillars of their relationship — even during stressful times. While trusting your partner means different things in different situations, in successful marriages spouses know they will protect each other, refrain from lying to each other, and act faithfully, no matter what challenges arise.

To honor your marriage, it is essential that you live with personal integrity while offering your respect and trust. To fight in a fair, balanced way, you must respect your spouse's emotional state, engage in a candid discussion of the problem, and hope for a resolution that might not come immediately.

For many couples, this is easier said than done. The following tools are designed to help you on your journey toward effective problem-solving, and ultimately, marital success.

1. Complain rather than criticize.

Instead of criticizing your spouse's character, focus on their behavior. Do not resort to calling the person names, or making generalizations about their being "mean" or "selfish." If you are frustrated about their spending, for instance, say, "You went over our entertainment budget this month" rather than exclaiming, "It's just like

---

56 Eggerichs, E. (2010). *CU Love & Respect Book & Workbook 2 in 1: The Love She Most Desires; The Respect He Desperately Needs.* Thomas Nelson Inc.

you to spend too much on things we don't need!" Avoid verbally attacking your spouse, which is simply not productive.

2. Steer clear of contempt.

Contempt takes criticism a step further and can be psychologically damaging. "What's the matter with you? You should know better, but obviously you don't!" is an example of contempt — not only does it exacerbate the issue, but it doesn't get to the root of the problem. Be diligent in keeping contemptuous remarks out of your marriage.

3. Listen carefully.

Your instincts will tell you to negate your spouse's complaints, but fight the urge to do so. Rather, listen carefully to what your partner has to say. Before you offer your own take on the situation, try to understand the issue. Ask your spouse clarifying questions as needed, and mirror what they are saying to show them you want to understand.

4. Avoid being defensive.

Defensiveness makes arguments even more heated. Making excuses for your behavior is no way to resolve a fight, even if you stand by what you are saying. If your partner says, "I think you spend too much time out with your friends," resist the urge to exclaim, "What else am I supposed to do? You never want to do anything outside the house!"

A healthy alternative? You could say, "How often do you think is too often? I would like to see if we can figure this out so that I'm home more often, but still fitting in some social time."

5. Commit to the discussion.

Gottman believes men are more likely to end disagreements prematurely, and reminds spouses that it's important to stay focused. Refrain from checking out during an argument, and strive to finish the discussion.

Sometimes starting the discussion is equally important. Married couples' unique takes on their financial situation are a major source of discord. Read how Julie and Sam addressed this topic in the case study below.

CASE STUDY — JULIE AND SAM

In a marital setting, financial issues aren't always rooted in the obvious. An argument might be sparked by a specific incident (spending too much on clothing, for example), but sometimes one partner's frustrations are related to the past rather than the present.

Five months into their relationship, Julie mentioned to Sam that she was carrying a $1,200 balance on a credit card. Sam was stunned. "How did this happen, Julie?" he asked.

In his view, Julie's spending was nothing short of irresponsible. Sam did not to know what to say, and offered to lend his partner the money to pay off her balance. This made Julie feel judged.

While their conversation proved difficult, Sam and Julie each made an effort to listen to the other's perspective. This prompted them to learn more about each other's financial habits and attitudes, and the differences between them began to make sense. Sam came from a stable, middle-class family. They lived within their means, bought used rather than new cars, and always paid cash.

Julie's family was more liberal in the way they spent their money. Her parents divorced when she was five, and while her mother did her best to budget her funds, money was always tight.

A few days after their conversation, Julie told Sam that she once had to help her mom make her mortgage payment. Sam felt much more empathy, while Julie learned why her partner preferred to avoid debt. She paid off what she owed, and she and Sam discussed the issue without making accusations, being overly defensive, or ending the conversation prematurely.

In fact, Julie now credits their talk about financial matters for their healthy perspective on not only budgeting, but also conflict resolution.

Are you familiar with your spouse's financial history? No matter how long you have been together, it can be very healthy to discuss the way your upbringing has affected your financial habits.

GET THE RIGHT TOOLS

Some spouses, no matter their income, are good at living within their means. Take Sheila — even with a relatively low salary, she always had money in the bank. She was one of five kids, having grown up with a stay-at-home mom and a schoolteacher dad, and frugality was practically her middle name. And yet, it seemed as though she never had enough money in the bank. Whenever Sheila made a purchase, she opted for the least-expensive option.

Before he and Sheila married, Mike used a simple spreadsheet to guide his spending. The couple eventually began to use it to track their joint finances, and it became clear that Sheila's response to any spending opportunity — that she and her husband couldn't afford the item in question — was rooted in fear. Seeing on paper that they actually *could* afford a better brand of clothing or the occasional restaurant meal gave Sheila a sense of freedom she had never before experienced with money.

A greater sense of freedom is just one benefit of maintaining a budget. Keeping a system to track where you and your spouse stand financially promotes transparency, teamwork, and trust.

TAKE A STEP BACK

Before you discuss a problem with your spouse, take a step back and check yourself. What issues, or "stuff," are you adding to the discussion? Reflect on the situation before you start the conversation.

Let's revisit a previous example: If you don't like how often your partner goes out with their coworkers or friends, ask yourself how their absence is affecting *you*. Perhaps you feel inferior to your spouses' friends and colleagues, or maybe the extra household tasks you must complete overwhelm you.

Once you recognize your feelings and understand where they are coming from, take a step back. Think carefully before you communicate, and speak in a way that will promote an open and honest discussion. Checking yourself in this way can yield a more productive outcome, ensuring you and your spouse take the time to listen rather than judge.

SURMOUNTING ROADBLOCKS

There are two elements to every conversation. The first one is the subject — the presenting issue, or the *what*. The second one is the process, the *how*, which refers to how you and your spouse make each other feel. Returning to the case of Alan and Dawn in Chapter 6, compare what Dawn said in frustration to this alternative response:

"I hate it when you spend so much time with your friends. You need to be home more."

OR

"When you spend so much time with your friends, it makes me feel like you don't want to be with me. I worry that I don't matter to you."

Which approach is more likely to garner a productive response? In the second version, by focusing on her feelings instead of making accusations, Dawn is encouraging her husband to participate in an open, honest conversation.

Now let's consider another example: a conversation I facilitated for Katherine and John.

CASE STUDY — KATHERINE AND JOHN

When John and Katherine sought help, the first comment they both made was, "All we do is argue." Katherine felt that John made everyone else a priority over her and their immediate family — particularly his family of origin. Both felt like they rarely talked the way they used to.

John was COO of a large multinational bank. Since he had moderate control over his travel, Katherine assumed he would plan to spend his time at home with her and the kids, who were eight and ten years old.

Dr. Lisa (to Katherine): What is it about John's schedule that makes you feel like there is not enough time? You admitted you know when he'll be home, so it would seem like you could make time for each other?

Katherine (to John): Well, there's your work, and I have to run the kids to activities almost every night. And there's your mother.

John (to Katherine): Mom does take some time when I am home. But what would you have me do, not take care of her? She is a widow, for God's sake.

Katherine: Some?! She's always calling you to do everything. She does not call your brothers and sisters, or even her neighbors — does she not understand you have a life too?

John: I never complain about your mother's cigarettes or cats. Do I complain when we go to her house? My mom is a wonderful person, and I think you and your mom could learn a lot from her.

Katherine: No doubt. According to her, I could be a better wife. And supposedly I am a terrible mother, or so she says every time I talk with her.

As you can see in their discussion, what began as a request to strategize effective ways to spend quality time together almost instantly escalated into a full-scale battle. John and Katherine's words, which defined the topic of their discussion, missed the root of the issue.

Upon further consult, it became clear that Katherine was trying to convey to John, "I don't feel important — I feel like you choose your mother over me. Please put me at the top of your priority list and pay more attention to me and the kids. I need your help and support." She didn't say it very clearly, but it was the best she could do at that particular time.

What you can learn from this case study is how important it is to check your reactions during an argument. Are you more interested in being "right" than you are in hearing what your partner is actually saying? Generally, in these instances, each person becomes defensive and argues their points without listening to the other. Even when your emotions take over, you must make sure to look your partner in the eye, listen to them, and consider not only their words, but also their feelings.

OVERCOMING THE URGE TO GIVE ADVICE

Perhaps there is enough openness in your marriage for you to share your feelings. Even so, many attempts at communication run smack into a roadblock — that is, the temptation to give advice. When Katherine would start to cry after an argument, John would make an effort to console her by saying, "Come on, don't cry. It's not that bad."

While John's intentions were positive, his advice was not a productive contribution to the conversation. From Katherine's perspective, John was telling her that she really shouldn't feel what she was feeling. And while John was simply trying to treat the symptom of a bigger problem, it was only when he became mentally present and stopped justifying his actions that he got past trying to "fix" Katherine's emotions and started making progress on their marriage.

It's normal to feel uneasy when your partner is expressing strong feelings, and this "advice" looks like a fast way to solve the problem. However, those feelings do not simply disappear. In fact, we tend to keep them with us, and they often resurface when we least expect them.

So instead of treating the physical symptoms of the problem, focus on discussing your spouse's feelings in an accepting way. "I guess I made you feel bad?" is a great place to start.

Remember, you are not an expert on your spouse's intentions. For this reason, you must be diligent about checking in with your partner on their emotions. Make this a regular part of your communication process.

A RETURN TO THE TWO-WAY STREET

Focusing on the topic area of a conversation instead of the underlying message — or trying to give advice or "fix" a problem by dismissing it — does not do much in the way of reconciliation. While there is plenty of communicating going on, it is not the kind that strengthens marriages!

You see, these roadblocks are related to a third problem. Many couples fail to recognize that in most arguments, both parties play a role and are "at fault."

Let's go back to John and Katherine. We've talked about John and what he could have done differently, but we haven't said much about Katherine's approach. And *her* approach was not effective either. She attacked John's mother — a surefire way to spark a negative reaction.

But as the conversation went on, Katherine became aware of the problem she'd created and asked John, "It bothered you when I criticized your mother, didn't it?"

Defensively, John retorted, "Yes. She's had a hard life, and I can't see why it bugs you that I take some time to help her."

Katherine tried to clarify her feelings with her husband's feelings in mind. "I realize that you love her, but I guess what I'm trying to say is that I need you around more. I really need your help."

Still angry, John snapped, "You don't know what rough times are."

Katherine, using tools we had discussed in previous sessions, answered, "What you just said really hurts. I need your help now, not a lecture."

And John, realizing what had happened, dropped the argument. "I'm sorry," he apologized. "Tell me what's really bothering you."

At this point, John and Katherine began to reconcile. They adopted effective communication techniques to ensure a smooth conversation.

That said, married couples must also be aware of a fourth roadblock in their communication: when one spouse conveys a message using words that do not match their tone of voice, gestures, or volume. "You must have had a hard day" can mean two different things, depending on whether it is spoken with tenderness or sarcasm.

This is because communication involves both words and the way we deliver our message. If your partner responds to you in a disjointed way — for example, if what they're saying doesn't reflect their tone — perhaps they are actually responding to another aspect of your communication, such as a delivery that maybe *you* didn't intend. By immediately defending yourself and saying, "I didn't say that! You always misunderstand me," you risk starting another argument. Instead, you should respond by checking in with your partner's feelings, and asking them, "Based on how you responded, I'm wondering what you heard me say and how it made you feel?"

To ensure effective communication *and* a seamless delivery, pause before you speak. More importantly, make sure your delivery aligns with the message you are trying to convey. Pay careful attention to your tone and body language, and should you or your spouse notice a discrepancy between what you are saying and how you are saying it, acknowledge the disconnect so you can move forward. This is essential to the health of your marriage.

KEY TAKEAWAYS

- At any one time, the brain is either receiving or sending information; it cannot do both simultaneously. When you listen to your spouse, make sure you are truly taking in what they are saying.

- No successful relationship is free of conflict. That said, you must acknowledge that there are two sides to every argument. Hold yourself accountable for your role in the disagreement, and accept that your spouse holds a different role.

- When your spouse expresses strong feelings, you may feel inclined to offer "advice" — but giving unwarranted advice isn't always helpful. Before you act, determine whether your partner really wants a fix. They may just want you to listen.

NEXT UP

Before delving into the final chapter of this book, reflect on what has already been detailed — that you are responsible for determining what is most important to you. How you choose to spend your time and energy reveals what you value most, showcasing your priorities both for yourself and to everyone around you.

Remember that when it comes to your values, your actions speak volumes. Use this information to be deliberate in the way you act, and to be mindful of your needs and desires. No matter how busy you are in the short term, do not forget to think about what you want your marriage, family, and career to look like in the long term.

9 NOW WHAT?

You rarely achieve finality. If you did, life would be over, but as you strive new visions open before you, new possibilities for the satisfaction of living.

—Eleanor Roosevelt

I want to reiterate that successful, happy marriages do not simply happen. They require attention, commitment, and skill, both individually and mutually. And, as described throughout this book, a successful, happy marriage is absolutely within reach — that is, if you put in the work and make your relationship a true priority in your life.

In *The Executive Marriage Solution*, I've shown you how to apply certain business practices to your marriage — opportunity costs, gap analysis, root cause analysis, and others. Additionally, we've explored the importance of *how* we communicate rather than simply *what* we communicate. Inherent in this emphasis of the process over the product is the fact that people hold unique perceptions of the same situation; and therefore, by revisiting the *how* from time to time, you and your spouse will be better-equipped to honor each other's maps, feel connected, and ultimately strengthen your relationship.

Remember that you can choose to take ownership for your decisions and behavior, and put in the work to enjoy a successful, rewarding marriage. With this in mind, I would like to provide ten guiding principles that come from the teachings in this book:

1. Take responsibility for the health of your relationship.
Like it or not, you and your spouse are responsible for the state of your marriage. Acknowledge that your beliefs, choices, and behaviors all play a role, and commit to being mindful. Make decisions that support your relationship.

2. Exhibit the behaviors you hope to see in your spouse.
If you want to be with a kind, considerate person, you too need to adopt these attributes. Lay the foundation for your marriage to succeed by acting in a way that makes you proud. Showing your spouse you love and respect them will help nurture the relationship.

3. Give more than you hope to receive.
Treat your partner the way you would like to be treated — and then go the extra mile. Be the example, even if you do not believe

your spouse is giving back what you are putting into the relationship. Live without any expectation of reciprocity.

4. Determine who you are.

Clarity about who you are and where you are headed brings feelings of purpose and fulfillment. Discuss what you want, and encourage your spouse to do the same. This will give you the framework to evaluate "what is next" in a mindful way.

5. Continue building your relationship skills.

Few couples put in the time to actively improve their relationship skills. Researchers explore the importance of doing so in the article "Which Relationship Skills Count Most?"[57] It's important that you work to continually strengthen your bond.

6. Advocate for your marriage.

Society conveys that spouses should consider divorce when things are no longer "fun" or "easy." Rather than accepting this outlook, try to view your marriage as the most important relationship you have. Remember that your union is sacred.[58]

7. Commit to your spouse.

Marriage is an investment not only in your partner, but also in your relationship. Even when things become difficult, honor the commitment you made to your spouse by putting in the work required to sustain a healthy marriage.

---

57 Epstein, R., Warfel, R., Johnson, J., Smith, R., & McKinney, P. (2013). Which relationship skills count most? *Journal of Couple & Relationship Therapy, 12(4),* 297–331.

58 Markman, H., Stanley, S., & Blumberg, S. L. (1998). Fighting for your marriage: Positive steps for preventing divorce and preserving a lasting love. *Family Court Review, 36(1),* 95.

8. Aim for personal growth.

The challenges we face help us learn and grow. Not only that, but couples who stay together through difficult times report that their marriages are happier and stronger.[59] Aim to improve yourself, and your marriage will improve too.

9. Learn from other successful relationships.

Those lacking in interpersonal skills and competencies tend to struggle sustaining a healthy relationship.[60] Most of my clients have not had role models in a happy marriage, and it shows.[61] Moving forward, remember that your example will give future generations a framework for their own success.[62] [63]

10. Remember that anything is possible.

If you want to enjoy a thriving marriage, you must put in the time to nurture your relationship. This will not occur organically any more than your next raise or promotion. Pinpoint your goals, and put in the work to achieve them.

Ultimately, the power to transform your marriage into a magnificent and fulfilling relationship is in your hands. It is the result of

---

59   Waite, L., & Gallagher, M. (2002). *The case for marriage: Why married people are happier, healthier and better off financially.* New York, NY: Broadway Books.

60   Epstein, R., Warfel, R., Johnson, J., Smith, R., & McKinney, P. (2013). *Which relationship skills count most? Journal of Couple & Relationship Therapy, 12(4), 297–331.*

61   Wallerstein, J. S., Lewis, J. M., & Blakeslee, S. (2001). *The unexpected legacy of divorce: A 25-year landmark study. White Plains, NY: Hyperion.*

62   Määttä, K., & Uusiautti, S. (2012). *Seven rules on having a happy marriage along with work. The Family Journal, 20(3), 267–273.*

63   Bumpass, L., & Lu, H. H. (2000). *Trends in cohabitation and implications for children's family contexts in the United States. Population Studies, 54(1), 29–41.*

the actions you take, for you have considerable power over your thoughts and attitudes.

You can choose how you feel about your spouse and how you manage the issues at play in your relationship. The two of you can take action to address the circumstances that culminated in distance and pain. Turning things around is your choice to make.

Clearly you would like success in your family and personal life, or you would never have read this book. Now that we've reached the end, you have two choices:

- You may put this book down and do nothing.

- Or you can do something different to improve your marriage and family relationships. If nothing changes, nothing changes.

As I noted in the Introduction, the tools detailed in *The Executive Marriage Solution* are only as good as their implementation. Without actually following through, it is probable that very little will change. At that point in the decision-making process you can decide that this is not the right path for you — or you can be more truthful and admit that you are not ready to make the required changes.

Simply know that you have the strategies at your disposal to make your marriage a success. It is possible to enjoy a healthy family and a successful career, as these two areas of your life can indeed thrive simultaneously. However, if you don't reconsider your approach, then nothing will change.

ON THE RESEARCH

1 *Green, C. H., Galford, R. M., & Maister, D. H. (2001). The Trusted Advisor. Simon and Schuster.*

2 *Johnson, D., & Grayson, K. (2005). Cognitive and affective trust in service relationships. Journal of Business research, 58(4), 500-507.*

3 *Tappin, S., & Cave, A. (2010). The new secrets of CEOs: 200 global chief executives on leading. London: Nicholas Brealey.*

4 *Ibid.*

5 *McCraty, R., Barrios-Choplin, B., Rozman, D., Atkinson, M., & Watkins, A. D. (1998). The impact of a new emotional self-management program on stress, emotions, heart rate variability, DHEA and cortisol. Integrative Physiological and Behavioral Science, 33(2), 151–170.*

6 *Centers for Disease Control and Prevention, National Center for Health Statistics. (2012). First marriages in the United States: Data from the 2006–2010 National Survey of Family Growth. US Department of Health and Human Services.*

7 *Martin, T. C., & Bumpass, L. L. (1989). Recent trends in marital disruption. Demography, 26(1), 37–51.*

[8] *Fein, E., & Schneider, S. (2007). The Rules (TM) for marriage: Time-tested secrets for making your marriage work. New York, NY: Grand Central.*

[9] *Roth, K. E., Harkins, D. A., & Eng, L. A. (2014). Parental conflict during divorce as an indicator of adjustment and future relationships: A retrospective sibling study. Journal of Divorce & Remarriage, 55(2), 117-138.*

[10] *Hetherington, E. M., Cox, M., & Cox, R. (1985). Long-term effects of divorce and remarriage on the adjustment of children. Journal of the American Academy of Child Psychiatry, 24(5), 518–530.*

[11] *Centers for Disease Control and Prevention, National Center for Health Statistics. (2012). First marriages in the United States: Data from the 2006–2010 National Survey of Family Growth. US Department of Health and Human Services.*

[12] *Cherlin, A. (2009). Marriage, divorce, remarriage. Cambridge, MA: Harvard University Press.*

[13] *Gottman, J. M. (2014). What predicts divorce?: The relationship between marital processes and marital outcomes. Hove, UK: Psychology Press.*

[14] *Glieberman, H. A. (1981). Why so many marriages fail. US News & World Report, 7, p. 54.*

[15] *Ibid*

[16] *Tappin, S., & Cave, A. (2010). The new secrets of CEOs: 200 global chief Executives on leading. London: Nicholas Brealey.*

[17] *Carter, L., & Minirth, F. (2004). The Anger Trap: Free yourself from the frustrations that sabotage your life. Jossey-Bass.*

[18] Hawkins, A. J., & Fackrell, T. A. (2011). *Should I Keep Trying To Work It Out? Sacred and Secular Perspectives on the Crossroads of Divorce. Brigham Young University Studies, 50(2), 143-157.*

[19] Sikora, M. (2000). *Trying to recoup the cost of lost opportunities. Mergers and Acquisitions, 35(3), 12–15.*

[20] Zimmerman, J. L., & Yahya-Zadeh, M. (2011). *Accounting for decision making and control. Issues in Accounting Education, 26(1), 258-259.*

[21] Ucbasaran, D., Shepherd, D. A., Lockett, A., & Lyon, S. J. (2013). *Life after business failure: The process and consequences of business failure for entrepreneurs. Journal of Management, 39(1), 163-202.*

[22] Durlauf, S. N., & Blume, L. (Eds.). (2008). *New Palgrave dictionary of economics. Basingstoke: Palgrave Macmillan.*

[23] Palmer, S., & Raftery, J. (1999). *Economics notes: Opportunity cost. BMJ: British Medical Journal, 318(7197), 1551.*

[24] Durlauf, S. N., & Blume, L. (Eds.). (2008). *New Palgrave dictionary of economics. Basingstoke: Palgrave Macmillan.*

[25] Valenzuela, S., Halpern, D., & Katz, J. E. (2014). *Social network sites, marriage well-being and divorce: Survey and state-level evidence from the United States. Computers in Human Behavior, 36, 94-101.*

[26] Manning, J. C. (2006). *The impact of Internet pornography on marriage and the family: A review of the research. Sexual Addiction & Compulsivity, 13(2–3), 131–165.*

27 *Dedmon, J. (2002, November 14). Is the Internet bad for your marriage? Online affairs, pornographic sites playing greater role in divorces. Press Release from the Dilenschneider Group, Inc.*

28 *Owusu, G., O'Brien, P., & Shakya, S. (2013). The role of service quality in transforming operations. In Transforming Field and Service Operations (pp. 153–165). Berlin: Springer.*

29 *Collins, J. C., & Porras, J. I. (2005). Built to last: Successful habits of visionary companies. New York, NY: Random House.*

30 *Eisenbeiss, S. A., Van Knippenberg, D., & Fahrbach, C. M. (2015). Doing well by doing good? Analyzing the relationship between CEO ethical leadership and firm performance. Journal of Business Ethics, 128(3), 635-651.*

31 *Frost, J. (2014). Values based leadership. Industrial and commercial training, 46(3), 124-129. Sheehan, 2000.*

32 *Kraemer, H. M. (2011). From values to action: The four principles of values-based leadership. John Wiley & Sons.*

33 *Doherty, W. J. (2013). Take back your marriage: Sticking together in a world that pulls us apart. New York, NY: Guilford Press.*

34 *Ibid.*

35 *Frost, J. (2014). Values based leadership. Industrial and commercial training, 46(3), 124-129. Sheehan, 2000.*

36 *Galley, M. (2008). Basic elements of a comprehensive investigation: Three steps and three tools that organize and improve your problem solving capability. ThinkReliability. Retrieved from http://www.thinkreliability.com/pdf/root-cause-analysis-article-basic-elements.pdf.*

37 Conger, S. (2015). *Six sigma and business process management. In Handbook on Business Process Management 1 (pp. 127-146). Springer, Berlin, Heidelberg.*

38 Ketola, J., & Roberts, K. (2003). *Correct!, prevent!, improve!: Driving improvement through problem solving and corrective and preventive action. Milwaukee, WI: American Society for Quality Press.*

39 Heuvel, L. N. V. (2005). *Root cause analysis handbook: a guide to effective incident investigation. Rothstein Associates Inc.*

40 Latino, R. J., Latino, K. C., & Latino, M. A. (2016). *Root cause analysis: improving performance for bottom-line results. CRC press.*

41 Rasiel, E. M., & Friga, P. N. (2002). *The McKinsey mind, understanding and implementing problem-solving tools and management techniques of the world's top strategic consulting firm. New York, NY: McGraw Hill.*

42 Gottman, J., & Silver, N. (2015). *The seven principles for making marriage work: A practical guide from the country's foremost relationship expert. Easton, PA: Harmony.*

43 Vuchinich, S. (1999). *Problem solving in families: Research and practice (v.13). New York, NY: Sage.*

44 Rabe, C. B. (2006). *The Innovation killer: How what we know limits what we can imagine—and what smart companies are doing about it. New York, NY: AMACOM, a Division of the American Management Association.*

45 *Barry, C. (2011). Lean marriage tips II: Using 5-why analysis and fishbone diagrams for problem-solving. Retrieved from http://blog.minitab.com/blog/real-world-quality-improvement/ lean-marriage-tips-ii.*

46 *Gottman, J. M. (2014). What predicts divorce?: The relationship between marital processes and marital outcomes. Hove, UK: Psychology Press.*

47 *Covey, S. (1989). The seven habits of highly successful people. New York, NY: Fireside/Simon & Schuster.*

48 *Gottman, J., & Silver, N. (2015). The seven principles for making marriage work: A practical guide from the country's foremost relationship expert. Easton, PA: Harmony.*

49 *Korzybski, A. (1993). Science and sanity: An introduction to non-Aristotelian systems and general semantics (5th ed.). Englewood, NJ: International Non-Aristotelian Library.*

50 *Goldhaber, G. M. (1993). Organizational communication. Madison, WI: Brown & Benchmark.*

51 *Ibid.*

52 *Ibid.*

53 *Gottman, J., Gottman, J. M., & Silver, N. (1995). Why marriages succeed or fail: And how you can make yours last. Simon and Schuster.*

54 *Gottman, J. M., Gottman, J., & Silver, N. (2015). The seven principles for making marriage work: A practical guide from the country's foremost relationship expert. Harmony.*

55 Burgoyne, C. B., Reibstein, J., Edmunds, A. M., & Routh, D. A. (2010). Marital commitment, money and marriage preparation: What changes after the wedding?. Journal of Community & Applied Social Psychology, 20(5), 390-403.

56 Eggerichs, E. (2010). CU Love & Respect Book & Workbook 2 in 1: The Love She Most Desires; The Respect He Desperately Needs. Thomas Nelson Inc.

57 Epstein, R., Warfel, R., Johnson, J., Smith, R., & McKinney, P. (2013). Which relationship skills count most? Journal of Couple & Relationship Therapy, 12(4), 297–331.

58 Markman, H., Stanley, S., & Blumberg, S. L. (1998). Fighting for your marriage: Positive steps for preventing divorce and preserving a lasting love. Family Court Review, 36(1), 95.

59 Waite, L., & Gallagher, M. (2002). The case for marriage: Why married people are happier, healthier and better off financially. New York, NY: Broadway Books.

60 Epstein, R., Warfel, R., Johnson, J., Smith, R., & McKinney, P. (2013). Which relationship skills count most? Journal of Couple & Relationship Therapy, 12(4), 297–331.

61 Wallerstein, J. S., Lewis, J. M., & Blakeslee, S. (2001). The unexpected legacy of divorce: A 25-year landmark study. White Plains, NY: Hyperion.

62 Määttä, K., & Uusiautti, S. (2012). Seven rules on having a happy marriage along with work. The Family Journal, 20(3), 267–273.

63 Bumpass, L., & Lu, H. H. (2000). Trends in cohabitation and implications for children's family contexts in the United States. Population Studies, 54(1), 29–41.

DEDICATION

I dedicate this book to the executives, clients, and couples who have inspired *The Executive Marriage Solution*. Your journeys have paved the way for other executive couples, and for this I thank you.

Special feelings of gratitude to my best friend and loving husband, who has unceasingly supported every pursuit that might propel me toward my dream.

To my kids — thank you for your patience regarding Mommy's early-morning and all-day Saturday writing sessions that often got in the way of our fun time. May this be a step toward more weekends together.

I also dedicate this book to the friends and colleagues who encouraged me to write. Your recognition that this work will make a positive impact means the world to me — even if only one marriage succeeds with the help of the *EMS*.

ACKNOWLEDGMENTS

First and foremost, I want to thank the colleagues and executives who gave me feedback and served as a source of inspiration for this book. You allowed me to think beyond my initial hypotheses and transform this manuscript into a path from which others can approach their marriages. Your time and insights were invaluable.

I also wish to thank my editors for their substantial proofing and guidance to expand the thoughts in my head into substance on paper.

Finally, I would like to give special thanks to SPS, ER, and CB — I had no idea where this journey would take me when I signed on for this writing journey in June 2015.

ABOUT THE AUTHOR

I am Dr. Lisa M. Webb ("Dr. Lisa"), business consultant and licensed clinical psychologist and the author of _The Executive Marriage Solution_. As President and CEO of <u>Body & Mind Consulting</u>, _I guide executive couples and families in their effort to reconnect._

What does it mean to "reconnect"? It could mean any number of things. Many executive clients contact me after a long affair with their work life—or perhaps with another person. Others simply feel misunderstood, and are hoping for a solution-based, strategic approach to rebuilding their marriage. I believe executive clients can acquire new ways of thinking, feeling, and behaving—ways that lead to lasting change.

I like to think I know a thing or two about sustaining a long-term relationship. I have been married to my husband for over 20 years, and we live outside Nashville, Tennessee with our two school-age children and a pair of rambunctious cats. But my career background is equally relevant.

While earning my doctorate, I originally planned to work in clinical practice. However, metrics, quality management, and strategy quickly proved most exciting to me. I attempted to integrate these facets of business into my profession.

But it took some time before I began working with executives and incorporating business strategies into my practice. My colleagues told me business and psychology were mutually exclusive. Clinician peers said, "Leave business to the business types—be a clinician or find yourself a research gig." Meanwhile, C-suite friends said, "You don't fit here, either. Nobody in business is going to take you seriously. Even if someone needs what you have to offer, they won't come to you. They won't want to see a shrink."

So I went back to school and got an MBA in International Business. The degree gave me a ticket to sit at the executives' table without being dismissed as a mere "shrink." Fast-forward several years, and I owe my success as a trusted advisor and author to my business background—along with my ability to apply success metrics within corporate strategy. I am thrilled to specialize in executive relationships, and proud to have combined my strengths in *The Executive Marriage Solution*.

WORK WITH DR. LISA

In my over two decades' experience working with executive couples and families, I have come to realize we are all capable of achieving work-life balance—that is, of finding success in both our relationships and in our career. To assist in this effort I developed a specialty concierge practice that accommodates select executives and their families in their effort to reconcile after infidelity or longstanding marital disconnect. These exclusive 1:1 couples' weekends and group couples retreats are the forum where EMS principles are implemented "in action."

To schedule a confidential consultation with Dr. Lisa, or inquire further about her exclusive retreats, contact her office at Consulting Associates/Body & Mind Consulting at 615.310.1491. You may also email her at clientrelations@bodymindtn.com.

The Executive Marriage Solution
Transforming Boardroom Success into Bedroom Bliss
Dr. Lisa M. Webb

Copyright 2018, Robins Flight Publishing and Dr. Lisa M. Webb
Printed in the United States of America

Library of Congress Cataloging-in-Publication Data
Name: Webb, Lisa. |1970-
Title: The executive marriage solution: transforming boardroom success into bedroom bliss. / by: Lisa M. Webb
Description: Murfreesboro, TN: Robins Flight Publishing, 2018.|
Summary: Successful executives can use the knowledge that they use at work and apply it at home with resounding success in their personal relationships.
Identifiers: ISBN 978-1-7325032-1-2 (hardcover) |ISBN 978-1-7325032-2-9 (softcover) |ISBN 978-1-7325032-3-6 (ebook)

Classification: Business-Nonfiction. Communication-Nonfiction.
Subjects: Relationships. | Executive success. |Success in marriage. | Personal success. Personal transformation.

A Robins Flight Press Book
Substantive Editor and Proofreader: Madeleine Cohen
Production Editor: Megan McCullough
Cover Design: Angie Alaya

First Edition

www.ingramcontent.com/pod-product-compliance
Lightning Source LLC
Chambersburg PA
CBHW060555200326
41521CB00007B/579